after troy

TABAN LO LIYONG

2021 © Taban lo Liyong
All rights reserved

ISBN 978-1-928476-34-4
ebook ISBN 978-1-928476-35-1

Deep South
contact@deepsouth.co.za
www.deepsouth.co.za

Distributed in South Africa by
University of KwaZulu-Natal Press
www.ukznpress.co.za

Printed and distributed in South Sudan by
Amo Publishers, Main Campus, Juba University
amopublishers@gmail.com

Distributed worldwide by
African Books Collective
PO Box 721, Oxford, OX1 9EN, UK
www.africanbookscollective.com/publishers/deep-south

An earlier version of the penelopey section of this work
was published in the *African-American Review*

Text design and layout: Liz Gowans
Cover design: Nonkosi Matrose

Contents

INTRODUCTION

John Jackson

I am honoured that Taban lo Liyong has asked me to write
an introduction to his poem *after troy*. Much of my 40 years of
teaching Classical Studies at Rhodes University was devoted to
Homer and Aeschylus, who presented superbly the heroes of the
Trojan War and its aftermath. Reading *after troy* has extended the
great adventure of my reading the traditional Greek texts. While lo
Liyong's book-length poem contains much that is familiar from the
classical accounts, it offers some startlingly new perspectives and
interpretations.

What follows here is an attempt to summarise the basic stories
of the two dynasties – not an entirely straightforward task since
even in antiquity the accounts of the same story could vary quite
considerably.

****

It is hard to imagine ancient Greek and Roman literature without
the war between the Greeks/Achaeans and the Trojans (the "Trojan
War"). Memories of this war inspired the two mighty epics
attributed to Homer, the *Iliad* and the *Odyssey* (the first works of
"western" literature) as well as a great many works in a variety of
genres over the next centuries. And yet it is very unlikely that a
single author named Homer composed these poems, or that they
were originally actually "written". If such an individual existed,
he was probably a compiler and editor of songs that had evolved
over three centuries before him – with each minstrel adding his
own improvisations. Was there historically a "Trojan War" or
indeed a "Troy"? Oddly, the answer is probably "yes". In the
late 19th century an unscientific amateur archaeologist (Heinrich
Schliemann) was almost certainly correct in claiming that he had
uncovered Troy, although what he thought was Troy – the city
of King Priam – had been built centuries earlier. A more likely
candidate was a set of ruins from violent destruction not quite so
far underground.

That some Greeks fought a war against Troy about 3000
years ago, need not be doubted. And the story that the news of

the Greeks' eventual success was conveyed within hours over hundreds of kilometres by a succession of beacon fires on hilltops, is also likely to be true.

The causes of the real war were presumably the ones that apply to any period of history: competition over trading routes, the desire for more land and mineral resources… But the focus in Homer and Greek literature has much more to do with individual people and the forces which drive them, especially love, lust, jealousy and revenge.

…Once upon a time a Trojan prince, Paris/Alexander, son of King Priam and Queen Hecuba, was visiting Sparta in Greece, where he was generously entertained by King Menelaus. Far from thanking him for his hospitality, Paris returned to Troy together with his host's wife, the famously beautiful Helen. Earlier there had been suitors for the hand of Helen. In a gentlemanly way these suitors, including Odysseus, had made a pact that should the one fortunate enough to be chosen be in difficulty, they would all come to his aid. Now that moment of difficulty had come. A confederate expedition, conveyed by a thousand ships, was led by Menelaus' brother Agamemnon.

The expedition was in trouble even before it had reached Troy. At Aulis the fleet could not continue – either there were no winds or the winds were too strong (the traditions vary). The goddess Artemis would not allow the fleet to proceed until Agamemnon had sacrificed his own daughter, Iphigeneia. This slaughter was not forgotten by his wife Clytemnestra.

And if any Achaeans, like some Britons in August 1914, thought the war would be over very soon, they were mistaken. For ten years they encountered one appalling problem after another as they besieged Troy, including the fact that their best warrior Achilles, because of some personal affront, refused to fight: Achilles sulks for several books of the *Iliad*. In the end the ever-wily Odysseus came up with the plan of constructing a huge wooden horse, into the belly of which were loaded a group of Achaean warriors. It was left outside the walls, and the unsuspecting Trojans dragged it inside their city. When all was quiet, the warriors inside opened the trapdoor, climbed out, and that was the beginning of the end.

For many Achaeans the victory at Troy did not mean the end of their troubles. What happened to the warriors returning from Troy was apparently a common theme in epic poetry, but the *Odyssey* is the only epic poem on this subject to have survived. It describes Odysseus' ordeals over ten years, as well as encounters (mostly erotic) with females human and divine, as he made his way back to Ithaca in western Greece. There, 20 years after his departure, he was reunited with his faithful wife Penelope and Telemachus, an infant when he left, now a young adult. Among the first to recognise him was the family dog Argus, who died from joy at seeing his master again. The final battle for Odysseus was dealing with the "suitors" who had moved into his home, helping themselves to its resources and in other ways pestering Penelope.

Agamemnon's return was quicker but much less happy. His wife Clytemnestra's anger at Agamemnon's killing of their daughter Iphigeneia was intensified by the presence of Cassandra, daughter of Priam and Hecuba, one of Agamemnon's "trophies" of the war. The god Apollo had granted Cassandra the ability to foresee the future accurately. When she refused his advances, he could not retract the prophetic gift, but punished her by bringing it about that no-one would believe her prophecies. On the evening of their arrival Clytemnestra killed both Agamemnon and Cassandra. Of course Cassandra had foreseen this, but her warnings had gone unheeded. Clytemnestra's accomplice was Agamemnon's cousin Aegisthus, with whom she had been having an affair during Agamemnon's absence.

And when Menelaus confronted his wayward wife at Troy, did he kill her in a rage? Not at all. They returned to Sparta, and after a stop-off in Egypt, picked up life from where they had left off.

This is a strange story – a series of interconnected stories really – which may be difficult for modern readers to grasp, especially those who find it absurd that gods and goddesses take sides for outrageously selfish reasons. Yet the capriciousness of the immortals is an important part of the story even before Helen's departure for Troy. Helen's mother Leda, married to Tyndareus, was impregnated by the god Zeus, who for that purpose disguised himself as a swan. This meant that Helen and Clytemnestra were half-sisters: Clytemnestra's father was Tyndareus and Helen's was Zeus. Helen was thus half-mortal, half-divine. In Greek culture, the line between human and divine tended to be blurred.

Some parts of the narrative which go back long before Helen's departure for Troy, explain the driving force of revenge, especially from one generation to the next. Atreus, father of Agamemnon and Menelaus, had served a meal to his brother Thyestes, which (as was later revealed to him) consisted of his own children. The child who escaped inclusion in the casserole, Aegisthus, had his revenge on Atreus' son, his cousin Agamemnon: he would have needed little persuasion to assist Clytemnestra with that murder. Clytemnestra and Aegisthus were later murdered by her son Orestes, who was pursued by the Furies (the goddesses of revenge) for killing kindred blood. In killing Iphigeneia, Agamemnon had also been guilty of this sin. He was punished by the Furies through the agency of Clytemnestra.

The sequence of retributive killing was ended only after Orestes was put on trial. The jurors, consisting of mortals and deities, had to consider which was worse: killing a husband or a mother. Orestes was saved by the intervention of the goddess Athene, who "argued" that a mother was less important than a father since Athene herself had no mother, born as she was from the head of Zeus. The story ends with a final murder (technically not a revenge killing) when Orestes kills the warrior Neoptolemus (son of Achilles) who had been betrothed to his cousin Hermione (daughter of Helen and Menelaus), and marries her himself.

****

The story of Odysseus and his dynasty is covered in the *Iliad* and (most of all) the *Odyssey*, whereas that of the dynasty of Atreus is told in the tragedies of Aeschylus, Sophocles and Euripides. These plays were usually presented in sets of three, "trilogies". (Only one complete trilogy has survived, Aeschylus' *Oresteia*.)

Lo Liyong, in his "book 1" uses this kind of structure (*the ithaca trilogy*) for Odysseus and his family's part of the story. We are offered the perspectives of Penelope, Odysseus and Telemachus – in that order. In his "book 2" (*trials and tribulations in the house of atreus*) the focus is on five characters: Helen, Cassandra, Agamemnon, Clytemnestra and Orestes. It is the latter who has the last word in lo Liyong's poem.

His use of separate "books" for the two dynasties might at first suggest that he has treated them separately. But the way in which they are presented reveals many links between the two. For example both Agamemnon and Odysseus are faced with the death of a child. Agamemnon sacrifices Iphigeneia so that the expedition can proceed. Odysseus, in an attempt to avoid being involved in the war, pretends to be mad. But when his son Telemachus is about to be cut up by a plough, he drops the pretence in order to save his son, and joins the expedition. A further fascinating connection is made between Telemachus and Iphigeneia. Telemachus, resenting the fact that he was one of those who stayed behind while others went to war, envies Iphigeneia for accompanying the expedition. A scene which features prominently in three Greek tragedies is the mutual recognition between Orestes and his sister Electra after the murder of their father Agamemnon. In lo Liyong's text the recognition is between Orestes and his other sister, Iphigeneia, based on an alternative account (see below) which has her rescued from sacrifice.

Much of lo Liyong's raw material can be traced in Homer and the plays of Aeschylus, Sophocles and Euripides. His text, however, involves far more than just another look at familiar old material. He delves more deeply into the hearts and minds of the central characters than his classical sources do. The reader is presented with complexity at every level. Sometimes the words come directly from the character; at other times they come from others speaking about the character. With Odysseus and Telemachus the modern device of a "double" is introduced. Sometimes the characters themselves speak from beyond the grave. Sometimes the sense of complexity is intensified by contrasting registers of language ("a dog ... decides not to croak ... the dog yclept argus").

Lo Liyong's Odysseus turns out to be more anti-war than one might have imagined, although there are hints of this in Homer. Telemachus' relationship with the goddess Athene is especially noteworthy. Athene helps him to recognise his father when he comes home, and during his long absence Telemachus sees her as a parent figure. Lo Liyong, however, goes beyond the classical tradition in giving Telemachus strongly erotic feelings towards Athene. In a way the young man's desire for a goddess is a counterpart to the god Zeus' desire for the mortal woman Leda, which led to the conception of Helen.

In terms of number, women are given equality with men in lo

Liyong's text. Four of the eight central characters are women. Although their voices are heard in Homer, and even more in Greek tragedy, Taban lo Liyong's poem lays bare many more of their possible thoughts. It is surely significant that the first character encountered by the reader is Penelope. As in the Greek tradition, she has been waiting patiently and faithfully for her husband's return. But some of her thoughts are not exactly innocent and certainly not those which one would normally associate with the stereotyped dutiful wife. And when it comes to the quick-wittedness, craftiness and ability to take initiatives, for which Odysseus was famous, she surpasses him – which he accepts.

Lo Liyong's characters are not confined to the period in which they are thought to have lived. They move freely through classical antiquity, and several of them reflect on figures in the intellectual life of 5th and 4th century BCE Athens, the "classical age", especially the sophists, Socrates and Plato. The Romans feature too, mainly in connection with their founder Aeneas, a refugee from Troy. But the time travel ranges far beyond ancient times, and includes references to Michelangelo, Gaddafi, cameras and rockets. These are not merely gimmicks of the kind that some classicists desperately use to persuade others that their subject is still "relevant". Throughout lo Liyong's text the reader is constantly invited to connect past and present and to be in touch with beliefs and practices throughout the world. From antiquity there has been a tendency not to take too seriously an alternative version to the story of Iphigeneia's sacrifice, in which at the last moment the goddess Artemis rescues her and substitutes a deer. Yet lo Liyong gives much prominence to this tale. In his poem a variety of views is offered on the notion of "substitute sacrifice", including cynical ones, and connections made beyond the ancient Greek world include Abraham and Christian theology. Throughout the text, especially as it nears the end, many of the reflections by lo Liyong's characters become timeless and universal.

Nor are lo Liyong's characters confined to the Aegean or even the Mediterranean. The reader is transported all over the world, most notably to Asia and Africa. Among the striking motifs are the polarities: East-West, fair skinned-dark skinned, and civilization-barbarism: in his poem they first appear in the Aegean but soon seem to resonate throughout the world.

The characters in lo Liyong are also given the freedom to allude in a very modern, self-referential way to the texts on which their existence depends. Odysseus notes (one imagines with a wry smile) that one has to go to war "to generate the stories". "Why," asks Telemachus "is this family so poetry-genic?" Such references even include the technicalities of structure and punctuation. Telemachus tells Iphigeneia that her "chapter was neatly closed: mine had a comma, many quotation marks, and now these open colons of ours." The effect of such words is especially interesting, given that the original stories come from a culture that was oral.

Is there any specific "message" in this work that will impress itself on the readers? I believe that the poem is too finely nuanced for that. But by the end most readers will be persuaded of the need to take responsibility for their own actions, to view cultures in a more relativistic way, and to delight in our shared humanity.

book one:

the ithaca trilogy

I   the penelopey

circumspect penelope regards ragged odysseus

1

this one too has come, like the rest of them carpetbaggers, to try
  his luck
at impersonating my husband, the unfortunate mortal who was
  fated
to incur ancient poseidon's implacable wrath and run the gauntlet

i was a mere bride when i dressed him in his war gear, and
  through
tear-filled eyes, bade him goodbye to far-off not-to-be-mentioned
ilion, where he was to test his skill in deviously planning the death
  of foes

twenty years have now gone by, twenty long and weary years, in
  which
i had to deploy all art known to womankind to keep looking
  young, my
figure trim, wear the social public face well, and keep discourse
  high

i brought up his infant child single-handed from birth to bearded
  youth
i denied myself change whilst supervising his; had to be the loving
  caring
mother whilst also playing the suffering wife whose husband is
  missing in war

you cannot bathe a boy, look at art, make a shroud without
  thinking
anatomical or physiological: naughty thoughts passed through my
  mind
whilst weaving at the loom, idle thoughts; i lived, fended off,
  denied myself

he was my source of strength: he the pillar that supported the roof with its
joinery: to bolster my strength, i leaned on him, thus i withstood the siege
of icarius' daughter in her husband's hall: a greater test than helen ever knew

distasteful is his name, and so has he been, or encounters with him:
there are many in hades, dispatched by him or his tricks; there are many maimed in body or mangled in heart whose paths crossed his: we bathe in tears

but is this he?

2

look, look at him: this expanding contracting mystery man; now a foot
taller, now looking an ordinary greek; now filled with vigour, now an
exhausted worker, now looking like a god, now the despicable beggar, now fashionable

a man with parts: what does he want with me old as i am, widowed in my
eyes, a legend in the land of ithaca; surely there is more beauty with
youth, and in his talked-about conquests he would have erased the taste of our first love

a man with pasts: am i to join his collection of past loves; to be
narrated from port to port as he does with calypso and circe? as if i lack
suitors; let me ask you all: what have i got which the rest of my kind don't?

they say he has had nymphs and goddesses for passing time; what chance did i
then have to enchant him all this while, above the gods who promised him immortality,
except that being human, he chose old age with me?

used up by other women for twenty years, now he comes all shrivelled
up and expects me to ululate for him: haven't i got eyes; don't i have
self-respect and a reputation to keep, did i wait this long for a beggar?

yesterday he beguiled me with many a tale which brought tears to my eyes;
but i am used to shedding them now; besides it fits my role of suffering

waiter: but what if he is weaving a trap for my lonely heart?

yesterday i quizzed him, the beggar, in clothing odysseus wore
    when he went
to war: his recollection was faultless, especially the description of
    the pin
with a hound holding/ensnaring the dappled fawn: the story of
    our joint destiny

is this he, though?

3

i am tired of keeping faith with a dead man's empty bed, i might
    have had another
child now in this one-son-per-generation house; but my
    companion at night
is my wet pillow; groaning from side to side, awaiting news from
    passing strangers

sleep at last and immortal night have been balsam to crying and
    wearying day,
otherwise, stranger sitting like a statue, mine has been the life of
    longing for
an absent man; till i am now well-schooled in waiting and fending
    off.

i have prayed to artemis, goddess and queen, patron saint of mine,
    to take away
life from inside my heart for fear i would one day be saddled by a
    worse man
than odysseus who broke my hymen; i hope the goddess hears me

well, i suppose all good things never last that long; twenty years is
    a generation gone,
but mine were twenty years without a husband, of husbanding
    myself,
of growing up again, of second courting ending in this disaster

telemachus is becoming a man now: just because he has a beard he
    now assumes
he is boss around here and practises that disappearing act of his
    father's
without a word: he needs a father to take him in hand

this killer – the hero, i suppose – has decimated antinoos and the
    rest:
the cream of ithaca society that paid me court is dead; for antinoos
the generous giver, a silent tear; but now that they are dead, what
    choice have i?

an irate god could have envied me this endless merrymaking
    without
being odysseus: this one is sometimes too old, at other times he's
    quite a beau,
and now he sits there quietly in profile thinking what?

could it be he?

4

our old maid swears the great oath that he is who he is; telemachus
    urges that
i embrace him as his absent father; now popular opinion is
    growing in his
favour especially since there's no rival: do i have a chance to
    convince myself?

yesterday i invented another game for my pets to while away the
    tedium of waiting:
the stringing of absent odysseus' bow (with ease) and the shooting
of an arrow (no second) through all the twelve axes (with ease)

surely, these suitors that i know would have taken years working
    around that one
whilst feasting on pigs, sheep, bulls, which we have in abundance:
this place is too large, cold, silent without such a raucous group

now up comes this bastard (none of my accredited suitors), who
    has no spirit
of play and ruined it all by being literal and realistic: don't you
    have
make-beliefs where you come begging from, you bloodthirsty
    man?

titans, cyclops, gods can bend and string any bow any moment
    and shoot
straight: beggar, i have told them i wouldn't marry you; it wasn't
    the
strength of arm that was contested: but i was pitting my wits
    against theirs

my life had steadied into creating conundrums for my tame pets;
    for holding
a salon; theirs it was to glory in my beauty, to sing my praises, to
    bring
the latest news and fashions whilst awaiting my never-coming
    final choice

when i had gone through this batch, or when some of them had
   retired due to
old age or lack of heart, i had looked forward to the generation of
   telemachus
to contribute their youthful suitors to my legendary role, hoping i
   remained young

perhaps my time is up?

5

perhaps my time of freedom and reverie is up: for last night i had
a dream which
was more like a vision: odysseus embraced me the way he did
before going to war;
i was tense, my heart constricted, then the release of distillation,
and wet thighs relaxing

but i can't just deliver myself like that: i can't just let myself go:
with a
crafty man like odysseus, how can one be his bride without
acquiring a few of his
articles of trade, without subjecting him too to tests? now is my
turn:

there is the scar, of course, but a lady cannot ask any passing
stranger to show
her his thigh scar in public; telemachus needs a father, but he
cannot satisfy
his hunger by foisting his father figure on me for a husband

eurykleia the old maid knows me too well; when she says: "your
heart was always
mistrustful", she should have addressed odysseus: for the truth
holds for us
both; if it is he, then let the dappled fawn ensnare him by the olive
root

the gods are my witnesses, i have tried to be true to my name to
the last;
if this ragged beggar-murderer passes this test, then vagabond
though he is
i am duty-bound to take him to bed and call him odysseus back
from troy:

"honoured guest, let your bed be made outside the well-fashioned
chamber, that very bed that you built, let it be put outside for
you..."

"goddamn woman! what have you said just now? my bed, my
 solid bed

built on a living olive bole, with its deep living root? who has
 moved my bed?"
it is he, the child, he remembers the toy chamber he built around
 the olive
bole which he crafted into a bed on which we are to continue our
 game

does boredom now begin?

coda

"odysseus, husband, tired wanderer, come now, calm down, rest
welcome home to your wife, child and bed; the bed has never
    moved,
but how was i to know you if i didn't shift its position somewhat?

in my place, preyed upon by many claimants and elegant suitors,
    my only
defence has been my wits: not auguries, dreams, or the human-
    impersonating gods:
the gods led helen astray; romance led clytemnestra to murder"

(the pin that the beggar recalled and aptly described, alerted me
    we had a
hot potato in the palace; the bow was useless: telemachus almost
    strung it;
the scar was commonplace: but the solid bed, the toy he made in
    his youth ...)

now i am satisfied my odysseus is back
back to end my static penelopey:
the fawn who never released the hound's hold.

II   the odyssiod

i   gaunt and bloody handed odysseus cogitates
by the family fire

1

agenda: things that are to be done; things people plan to do:
hourly, daily, weekly, yearly, lifely
we all have our agendas: most of us plan by ourselves their
supervision and their carrying out;
but a few get it in their heads to incorporate others in their grand
designs, grand agenda

take this matter of king menelaus and his wife helen and their
disrespectful guest paris, for example:
an elderly man, with fewer vices than virtue itself, welcomes a
handsome youthful guest and guesses not
what the chemistry of youth and beauty in the unwatchful
husband's house may eventually lead to

sooner than later the prescription that spells disaster becomes the
order of the day and the beginning of national calamity:
especially in the realm of related principalities and leaders of
confederacies that can put many men and officers under arms;
now we have the achaians on this side armed to the teeth and the
ilion hosts on the other side ranged against them

and what is the achaian battle-cry? if odysseus of the fast mind and
intricate contrivance does not report for duty
the galleons shall never be boarded! wait a moment: is this my
war? are my bags of tricks weightier than fifty achilleses?
do kings depend less on their masters of the spear in the field but
more on the planning generals in headquarters?

2

this is the winter of good auguries for rich olive harvest, multiple
    lambing and shearing of the long woollen fleece,
and by royal diktat odysseus must leave his infant son, take his
    fighters away from domestic and economic engagements,
go be the central pillar in the planning of destruction of ilion and if
    possible lead the most daring raid that finally ruins her

don't i have my own agenda? no wife to husband well? are others'
    weaknesses now made grounds for disturbing my peace?
if in their agoras the windy philosophers know their duty they
    should have produced primers for wife-raising in their time-
    passing academies
why should ethics not be taught to girl children as well so that
    they know their house-wifery and how to fend off errant guests
    like my own penelope?

if they think it will be that easy to get my father's only son off his
    farm to venture out into the field of mars they have to think
    again:
this is my week of winter sowing, shearing of sheep, pruning of
    olives as well as supervising the raising of my infant son;
i understand a delegation is on the way: but i shall rise early, take
    my seeds and chemicals to stimulate growth and be gone

3

now, wonder of wonders, here they come, with my infant son
    telemachus brought hither by nurse
what on earth do they intend to do, placing my son on the direct
    path of the plough?
what: are they mad, placing innocent telemachus on the path of
    the plough?

if they think i shall cut my son and only child into two, then they
    have a thought coming.
if we all have to leave our fields, and wives, then let's all do so: no
    need to plough up a child
blood spilling is anathema to the gods and goddesses: neither
    helen nor paris is equal to my only son

4

in my family, like the ground nightjar, only one egg hatches per
  marriage or generation:
my father was an only son, only child; he in turn engendered only
  me without a sibling;
and i have this telemachus, there is no second before or after, to
  make me gamble

to say i dote on telemachus is to understate the truth, or utter a
  blatant lie;
i have to put on my war-gear and go to the front and generate the
  stories –
stories that will give telemachus some things to extend the line for:
  life is a pack of deeds retold

what an inheritance will be his if i do not devise the nooses that
  will entangle foes?
what an inheritance will be my living father's if i cut his grandson
  into two for maintaining a point against society?
what an inheritance will my wife and her people have, being
  married to a war-fearing in-law?

by not donning my war-gear at first bugle blow, i have raised my
  status and gauged my rank in the order of things,
now i know agamemnon of the deep brow, or achilles of the long
  bow, or blind prophet tiresias, are nothings
but poor substitutes for odysseus. selfish thoughts? well we all
  have our prides and prices

5

there she sits at the loom; looked at in profile, you can see that
   sturdy, taut and shiny facial skin –
only in japanese or chinese etchings and paintings do you find
   such features so deftly rounded off by the artist's skill;
only utamaro amongst masters knew how to capture those high
   cheekbones that genghis khan, timor and the mongolians spread

married to such a woman you had better be alert: king menelaus'
   wife from the steppes was a paragon of beauty any man would
   have loved to grace his palace,
she, the offspring of a swan and her mother, the mother who later
   bore king agamemnon's wife, are women that tragedies are
   crafted around
as for my own penelope, she was born of a king and a queen;
   palatial breeding she had enough of, besides i passed to her a
   few of my tricks

now i return to find my son wearing his first growth of beard: he
   has that youthful glow that college boys have; public exuberance
   and sophomoric bravado
time had elapsed enough for any ordinary western woman to have
   started shrivelling, wearing the crow's feet and hiding her age:
but not so my penelope: that oil skin under the yellow tinged skin
   glows with the sun, unlike her caucasian cousin's skin which,
   being porous, singes

6

years may pass, children may grow up, bulky, wise, married,
   widowed, childed, as the case may be
my child has expanded, he is tall, has bearing; he stands out in
   public; besides, his mentor and my father were around to fill the
   gap:
some qualities we get from both parents, others we acquire from
   growing up with mates, some we steal from our enemies: not
   everything is taught

how would he have fared at the front? has he been thinking of
   engagements in future wars? would he have preferred to be a
   ship's captain?
has he been crying for manly engagements or has he been glued to
   his mother's apron? did he have youth around him for a junior
   league?
the battle royal that is to engulf this house with all its joinery, is he
   prepared to take his rightful part in it? the testing time will tell

about my escapades on the return journey, would he have
   condoned my activities? would he have taken them as learning
   experiences?
there was calypso of the sweet music, there was circe of the
   enticing circles, we had to outwit the sirens as well as dupe
   cyclops of the singular eye:
would he have had moral scruples against blinding foes, jilting
   foreign mothers? does he know that to return may mean more
   snares than to go?

there she sits, and it is eleven o'clock at night; is this the time she
    has been keeping? is this how long they have been keeping her
    up?
what have they turned my house into? what have they been doing
    to my wife? depriving her of sleep? there was the shroud, of
    course
or does she have one particular lover who remains awake till
    everybody is asleep before creeping with her under the blanket,
    and then sleeps all day long

well, darling wife, sorry; tonight he will not come; if it was
    antinoos, then you already know his fate, if he was another, the
    same fate too
if previous nights had belonged to interlopers, then this particular
    night belongs to the rightful owner of property: from now
    onwards
it is going towards midnight, the bewitching time is here; with
    circe we started earlier than now; with calypso we would hear
    the second song

there is already the slackening of pace, yawning comes and is
    stifled; one suspects there will be a clearing of the phlegm soon
now i seem to see the escape of some words from her mouth; their
    purport seems to be portentous to whatever will be from now
    onwards:
"should your bed be moved from the bedroom to the verandah? it
    is cooler this time of year outside there, blessed father of my son"

8

"woman, what have you said just now? move my bed from the
   bedroom to the verandah out here? what bed are you talking
   about?
who could have moved my bed? who can move that bed and still
   remain with a bed? stop this joke; it is in bad taste!"
the live olive bole whose branches were crafted into our bridal bed
   was a snare for this very night; that private joke now deserves
   celebrating

"calm down; be calm tired warrior! tired traveller, calm down!
   father of telemachus calm down, my odysseus calm down
the olive bole bed has never moved; who could have moved it and
   remained with a bed, as you have just said? the bed cannot move
   but i had to move it somewhat
however, if you were in my place, besieged by the cream of ithaca
   gentry, how would you have fended them off?

"give us some credit also, you men; the way of the sword is the
   forward thrusting, backward cutting way: it is forward-backward
   all the time
what about the sly, sideways look, the underhanded way for
   wearing down the rock with dripping, with nagging, with
   repetition?
was homer wrong when he devised for me the shroud-making by
   daytime and its undoing by night? so simple, yet so effective!"

more like it: that's my wife: the girl i chose to measure my wits
    against: every son of his father is lucky who has a brain-teasing
    contestant-colleague at home
shortsightedly, i had thought she would get all the cues from me;
    little did i give her in the department of initiative-taking, or
    paradigm extension
yesterday she tested me on the arrow-shooting; i had thought
    she would follow it up with showing her my thigh scar; foolish
    man's pride

the buckle with its fawn-enticed hind i had worn all the war years,
    she had buckled me with it when i put on my war-gear
this was clue enough to her that i was no mere guest; the rest of the
    day's exhibitions were mere confirmations: we played the game
    of catch me if you can
every married couple has some secrets they know about: their
    first night together or the most endearing thing done on the last
    departure or last return

now where's that boy, the one and only that was engendered on
    the olive-bole bed? where's he whose face i had longed to see
    since i nearly ploughed him over?
i wish i had been here to husband my wife and raise my son; i
    wish we had had all our lives to ourselves instead of going to
    recover somebody's wayward wife –
war is a waster of lives; war's rationales had better be for
    substantial things like saving much territory, rescuing many
    people, bringing joy to many faces

10

does god mars have a hold on human and animal psyche? my
  young goats fight one another hornless, they practise mounting
  one another indiscriminately
do the gods love to bathe their hands in hot gurgling blood? do
  they love to feast on the smell of burning animal flesh and drink
  nectar to camouflage human blood?
do they know how ill war leaves human life? how flirty helen and
  her pulled-by-the-nose-boy paris became conveyors of youthful
  deaths to hades and ilion's fall?

well, violence has its logic: death-missed paris ran from the fight
  to go and sink his aroused manhood into his mistress helen of
  the thousand ships,
the slaughter of the war-fearers and stealers of soldiers' wives
  left at home, which are their rightful and rueful deserts, was the
  prelude to love-making my waist needed most:
twenty years have gone by, twenty anxious years when i missed
  the soft hands of the daughter of icarius, my patient ministrant;
  today is the day

tonight we shall love for love's sake; tonight we shall love to
  celebrate our survival; tonight we shall relive the experiences of
  our youthful lives;
tonight we are loving without the hope or desire to make any
  children; no designs upon one another; no plans for escape from
  her: she is no circe
"my dear penelope, let us make love to celebrate my homecoming,
  to celebrate our reunion; i am back home as strong as ever!"

coda

the rewards of departures are reunions:
the cold tears of departures are always wiped away
when the warm tears of welcome flow from the same veins

every departure deserves a return
every return deserves a celebration:
let us give ourselves to each other

ii   odysseus' double prepares for his first inland odyssey

1

i am the lord of ithaca, a small urban principality we give the name
    city to, like any settlement
in my youth i travelled the whole-crooked-shored land of greece
    till i learned that inland in sparta
there was the lordly icarius, a much famed king, with a daughter
    who graced his palace to the nines

the spartans are spartan as the saying now goes and in our
    philosopher-riddled land of greece
where one philosopher prattles his song in the agora and wins the
    popular cheer regardless
and the others, genteel and unkempt, lord it over the gentry's
    youth passing time in talking idleness

if she would practise spartan economy with our wares in our
    household too, then this would be the girl for me
we met with penelope, she would penelopey in my house as i
    odysseyed in the dark-rimmed sea
from the onset, i was already a wanderer, choosing my bride from
    the eastern shores, through aid of gods and men

when i made our bridal chamber in the olive grove, and wove the
    bed from a live olive bole, that was spartan already
when i told her to remarry only when our son came of age should i
    not have returned by then, we already had trust
when she feasted the would-be suitors on my bulls, it was the
    lesser of evils; she was buying time

2

when i look at her ankles as she lifts them up before putting them
  down especially after she has had her bath
i know i met with those ankles elsewhere, the same with that
  stately bearing which she carries so regally
and that fieriness when the temper comes upon her, did not
  calypso show it to me in her island? or who was it?

we each have one love in this world: the girl whose visage
  imprints itself, the girl whose voice you hear in your dreams, she
  whose hand imprint remains
faraway from childhood; then she disappears, and you are left to
  pick the last approximation who is made of parts,
of parts and fragments, the more parts the better chance of a
  penelopean and an odyssean marriage

so, sister penelope, i lived with the dream love for eighteen years
  before i married you, i lived with you twenty years away
now i am back for the third season of ordained conjugal living:
  i am condemned to go inland in the fourth quarter till my
  walking-staff oar is mistaken for a winnowing utensil
by a race unschooled in seafaring and only brought up cultivating
  grains

before my next trip, i shall have installed telemachus on the
  throne; he who had been practising his own telemachy
now needs to become a man, marry a wife, have our hallowed one-
  son-per-generation, and learn husbandry
a man should have a wife, a child, friends, parents, slaves and
  workers in order to fulfil his growth.

3

agamemnon, the lord of hosts is chief who belongs to the highest
   league; he's on our achaians' side as
priam is the lord of the trojans, our implacable rivals but of lesser
   civilization; they are trainers of horses as
we are breeders of beauties, practisers of hospitality, and
   harnessers of allies for fighting the common foe

the wind refuses to blow, year after year, children become boys
   and girls – girls become women; it is ten years
the auguries are consulted and their decree is heart-piercing: let
   the king cut the throat of his only daughter
and throw the carcass to the sea so typhon can release the all-
   important wind – wind that will blow our hosts towards troy

in another age when substitute sacrifices have been invented, one
   or two sheep could be used –
the king, sitting in council of war with all his generals, well armed,
   heard the augury and gave the orders
she, the king's daughter, who would have been a meet bride for
   my own telemachus, was cut to pieces: agamemnon is madder
   than me!

missing in war, assumed dead; widowed perhaps is what every
   soldier's wife hopes or fears would be her fate
there are also men who do not put on the soldier's uniform or
   aspire to the heroic life of hacking flesh
and those who worm themselves into the warm and spacious heart
   of a woman whose husband is at war with fierce foes

4

it was such a pair in clytemnestra – her name already tongue-
twisting and dissonant – and her cowardly man
who waited at home to hack the tired and retiring king
agamemnon now returning to his home supported by the
prophesying-cassandra,
walked to their grave like the tragic characters they were; in any
case the tale had to end

the lord of hosts, who agamemnon was, the *primus inter pares*, he
stood out head and shoulders above all others;
his word is just, his word overrules all others' whether spoken
first, middle or last just as when booties are gathered and shared,
and after he made the supreme sacrifice of ill-fated iphigenia,
when opportunity came he would chance upon another:

briseis, daughter of apollo's priest, filled with unbelievable
prophecies, briseis who may have resembled his daughter now
dead
he had to console himself with her; in any case, who was achilles
without the combined achaian forces?
the strength of arms, we know its importance and limitations too:
but the power of kings is to mobilise allies and warriors.

when the ground outside troy became a war arena, and priam
climbed the parapet to have helen
point out to him the gallant warriors on her husband's – sorry,
former husband's – side, that was pathetic
imagine a beleaguered king, reduced to spectator, and watching
his children's slaughterers pointed out to him by her who
brought this fire to troy!

5

take a kodak camera, load it with a video cassette and train it on
    the ramparts where father-in-law, a king
sits closely with his daughter-in-law, cause of the launch of the
    thousand ships, and also the coming wreck of troy,
capture the natural beauty of helen – beautiful like an aging swan,
    and the king, haggard like a stallion

does the man with a sharp mind who can see – who can see – what
    is at the back of the moon, or who can plan the trojan horse
care about the distinction between the good and the bad? when
    troy had to be breached, was it not what worked that prevailed?
what worked, efficiently, effectively? in the cave of polyphemus,
    was it not mine and my people's lives versus his?

if a love-sick lady – call her circe, or calypso – captures the jetsam-
    flotsam wanderer and keeps him
does she not think: as it came so would it also go, so make the best
    use of him as you can, *ubi sunt*?
even aeneas will one day leave queen dido to die on the pyre by
    the coast of muammar gaddafi's libya

should anybody shed tears when passing promises by passing
    strangers used as passing stratagem for passing time
get broken or auto-disintegrate when their times are up: same
    when acts done during war are judged
by laws that are not civil: acts of engagement, as well as when
    agreements exacted under duress, lapse with time

when one belongs to the sicilian brotherhood, sworn to the greater
    oath of omertà, surely the world now belongs to two:
the sworn brotherhood, and those they have sworn against: the
    ethical lyre is now broken, five strings sound, two do not:
we need another code of ethics: the post-socratic ethics of the
    sophists: lawyers win cases through technicalities

in all my life, the only thing i did not countenance was to have my
    intelligence abused or underestimated:
would penelope reveal herself to me? would she still seek for
    proof of my odysseusness, or would she lie?
now i see her beckoning: to speak, penelope is clearing her throat
    of phlegm: let her speak

"stranger, tired stranger, would you like your bed moved to the
    verandah where the wind blows?"
"what foolishness is that? what have you just said? move my bed?
    a bed made from a living olive bole?"
after my outburst, i have realized she is cleverer than me, she
    trapped me; i fell into the trap and also outbursted!

so i am still capable of getting angry, getting hurt, being vain, and
    showing off what i know, still human am i,
and why not? we have one love; to him or her we abase ourselves,
    we debase ourselves, we go for shriving, we confess
god walks in a woman; god walks in a man; the avatars of god are
    many, asian religions are adept at making them

he-who-was-much-prayed-for is my other name, given to me
by grandfather; wait a moment, isn't that another's occasional
handle? he who was entreated for;
for what was i entreated? to please my father and mother? to
extend my granddad's life? to be the gods' vessel?
or to be the effective tool for the destruction of ilion and cause of
headaches along the way on my return journey?

return home to me; was it to be to the olive-bole bed? would
penelope be strange after circe and calypso?
would i hold her gently, or use *force majeure* in grabbing her to bed
as one wrestles down an opponent?
don't i have words for my father laertes, nurse eurycleia, eumeus
and philoetius, leave alone dead argus?

the ruse of making a burial shroud for laertes kept penelope busy,
as well as doing the time honoured thing
did dad laertes not have a place in my thought as i went forth –
like his representative – or fought as i came home?
argus waited till he beheld me; eurycleia shrieked when she
recognized the old boar's wound on the right thigh – human
qualities – quite legitimate

when i shut eurycleia's mouth, that was prudent; tactics of war:
any premature revelation would have proved fatal
after the journey to hades, and having learnt of what aegisthus did
to agamemnon with treacherous clytemnestra
a misdeed which orestes will correct to avenge his father's death
on his mother and her craven suitor

being brought up very well is a burden, as civilization is a burden,
the final confrontation here was not for penelope's sight
two-generations-tutor eurycleia had led her away and under lock
and key put her on valium
only to be woken after the carnage and the smell of intoxicating
blood was scrubbed clean from the palatial stage: greek drama
taught many a lesson

coda

now, i have seen telemachus at war: he alone almost strung the
   bow: the bow everybody regarded with awe
he helped decimate his mother's suitors, my treacherous rivals; i
   can report to agamemnon that my son
has avenged the wrongs the stay-at-homers meted out in my
   house, as his son orestes would do to his enemies

III   the telemachy

i   youthful telemachus carves out a role for himself

1

there they are, together at last, bridging a twenty year old
  separation
this one to my right is at her wonted place, seated with the loom
  before her, trying to do some weaving or unweaving
that one is lying on his side like michelangelo's god, exhausted
  after a hard week's work

here they are together at last: the man whose fathering of me
  passed unattended
and the woman who scant gave me any upbringing, engaged as
  she was in fending off suitors and loiterers;
they are supposed to be reunited: he from his famous odysseying,
  and she from her penelopeying waiting game

my parents make a nice study in contrasts: he coming home
  looking like a carpetbagger;
she, always the beauty, looking as radiant as ever, especially after
  a face cream or two;
he who had to arrive in disguises; she who had needed no
  disguises ever

2

here is he whose return was marked by the death of odysseus'
    long-memoried dog argus from cardiac arrest, after a twenty
    year wait,
he who had to muffle our common wet-nurse's excitement when
    she saw the scar the wild boar had gashed on her master's thigh
    by the groin,
she to whose wan face the blood had flushed and the scarlet had
    shown through the heavy makeup

here is he who seemed to know the detailed whereabouts of the
    family arsenal and how to command the servants masterfully
when he called me "boy" it sounded to my ear like "son", a sound
    i seem to have heard in a dream
there's that glow you get when patted on the bum by dad: it
    tingles right to the core!

it was athena who had told me who the stranger could be but i still
    awaited further revelations
with that grey-eyed lady who is a master of myriad disguises, any
    semblance she puts on may be real or unreal
i shall sit here in this penumbra, and with mother watch to
    dismiss; or with father be circumspect, till the snake is out of the
    hole

3

they say my would-have-been age mate, the fated daughter of
clytemnestra, iphigenia by name, had to die the early death i too
should have faced
but my father was not too keen to go to recover a man's flirty wife
(of that distasteful name) if that man could not husband her well
the madness he had to put on almost cost me my life: sowing salt;
they brought me as a better seed and dared father to furrow me!

at least i have a father who hates war waged for trivial matters like
honour and prestige, boring old potentates with beautiful young
wives
had better never leave young princes from another race alone with
their wives; you can never tell what cupid's arrows can do;
the small heart in its cavity threatens to burst when the chemistry
of desire sends the blood gushing to the eye and breathing
becomes constricted

my father is the famed argives' master disguiser or unmasker but
he had rivals too: palamedes, he who took me from eurycleia for
mad slaughter
i now believe that the spirit he fell into when slaughtering those
unarmed suitors was of an avenging angel meting out justice
men who are half men; preferers of making merry with wives of
soldiers braving cold and deprivation in the defence of territory,
possession or honour

4

sympathies, age mate slaughtered so the wind that would take the
   argive galleon to the erasure of ilion would blow –
history records your death as the single event that was needed for
   everything else to happen: the fulcrum on which the lever rests
your chapter was neat and closed (or so thought your father);
   mine has commas, semicolons, colons and question marks; open
   ended, so opine i

childhood: did i have any? with a society girl for a mother, forever
   powdering her nose and changing her dress?
childhood: did i have one? left as i was to a common wet-nurse
   from whom i was snatched and taken for ploughing over;
childhood: was there one to talk of apart from the itinerants'
   stories about a crafty warrior taking his time returning, sampling
   the islands and their specialities

clytemnestra's daughter, you at least went to the war front, and
   saw action, even if it was your undoing: first victim of martial
   confrontations
and i, penelope's son, have been dying a domestic death,
   smothered between wet-nurse and mother, when she had time
nearly ploughed over at birth, i have lived in death's shadow;
   the only action i have been grudged is the slaughter of some
   domestic captives too foolish for their own good

now that mother's favourite, antinoos, is dead, he who was wont
   to give me white and red grapes, apples and olives, in season
now that their souls are gone to hades, and their relatives are
   coming to cart their earthly remains for pyre burning and funeral
   services on the morrow
i suppose this winner will be declared my father and the husband
   of my mother: something the stay-at-homers had never thought
   of

a war ended in faraway fabulous ilion, a town left in ruins of
   history, like iphigenia its precursor, and the master-stroke
   manufacturer goes peregrinating
whatever thoughts of me did he have? with my teen years coming
   to a close, could he not have sent for me to meet him in such and
   such a place?
a war ends, husbands with agendas hurry back home unless some
   goddess has sent evil winds to steer their ships off course, my
   father loiters in the middle world sea

a war ends; mother receives missives from the rialto and wharfs,
   of sightings of her man between circe and calypso
did they who carried tales homewards not also take false reports
   to the hardhearted man too? he trusted in his wife completely,
   or never cared
with antinoos being favoured, did tongues not wag? with all the
   tales of the palace goings-on, could not a drop of jealousy sting
   him to hurry back home?

6

a war ends. all creatures are preserved: grandfather is kept alive
  so the ruse of the shroud could have some use and meaning, to
  prove the rule
was it a trick of fate? keep his death a daily expectation so the
  suitors, blinded to their fate, looked forward to possessing, and
  not losing her?
a war ends; the bride knits the names of the meddlesome suitors
  for the angels of death to copy till they had learnt them all by
  heart

a war ends, and a dog older than me gasps his last because a
  charismatic stranger has made his dramatic entrance to town;
a war ends, the eternal shepherd of greek stories, kept alive all
  these years, springs to action energetic as ever, with the strength
  of his arm intact
a war ends, our common wet-nurse is still alive, ministering to the
  stranger with the tell-tale thigh scar, too close for others to see,
  and ready to shout

they say she of many disguises is a goddess; her voice is sweet
  and caressing, it lies between a boy's and a man's, is deep and
  rasping, honey-coloured
when i look into those eyes i find myself pulled therewards, or am
  transfixed in the same place; at other times my heart seems to
  stand still
if she were a woman, only she could have absolute power over my
  being; as it is, let her say "come" and i am bound to follow at a
  trot

7

in the agora where the talkers meet they doubt the divinities, what
    with so many old tongue-waggers overstaying their welcome in
    the gymnasia:
they are likely to get lost between the old teachings and those of
    fertile minded asiatics or westerners bent on short-cuts from the
    italian foot and calf
after seeing this goddess, i swear: any fast talker who denies the
    existence of goddesses and angels will incur my eternal wrath

when athena told me a stranger was coming and i should prepare
    to await his arrival with all due preparations
out of love for her, i was ready to go beyond the call of duty; it is
    not every eighteener who is favoured by a goddess; besides, you
    never know... one day, you never know
the love i never received at home was now showered on me, me a
    fatherless boy, me a neglected son of my mother; athena is my
    mother, and is my love, the only one

athena sent me to visit my grandfather laertes in the village where
    he had been tucked away by my society mother; to be out of the
    way?
these are my only parents who taught me manhood, filialty,
    dutifulness: she of the straight nose bridge, and he already
    bedridden;
there was uncle diomedes, too, he who had known my father in
    their youth, who was in that hunt of the boar, and fought at ilion;
    he took me in as a son

8

they have stayed like that the whole evening; i even think when i
    went woolgathering and sweet athena glued me to her, i must
    have slumbered
this tedium is getting on my nerves: the whole palace is an open
    morgue and these living corpses are still parrying, trying to see
    who will blink first
he has been playing a solitary game of draughts the whole
    evening, whilst she has been playing at weaving-unweaving the
    eternal shroud, perhaps this time for real

one of them is likely to break the silence; i wonder which of them
    will do it first:
i see the woman, my mother, yawning; it is past her sleeping time
normally, by now, the suitors would have retreated to their
    dormitories and she would be completing the unthreading of the
    day's piece of shroud

this black-letter day has them all dispatched to hades, and perhaps
    some straggling souls are still wandering, dazed, this side of styx
now that death has been introduced into this house, poor woman,
    you had better make the shroud for real; your father-in-law
    hasn't much time left
it won't be long before grandfather packs up and goes to the vale
    of happy spirits: about time too for aimless old age is boring

9

the famous shroud will not be experiencing any untying tonight;
    this is the new dawn night
the woman, my mother, will break the ice first, if i know my
    mother, and am my famed father's son:
she has to play the host: give the stranger a place to lay his
    exhausted bones and leave further explanations for the morrow

what was that i've just heard? mother coughed and asked the
    stranger about a bed?
i had always suspected there was a story about that immobile bed:
    staying put like everything else in this house, till tonight
did mother ask the stranger if his bed could be moved out here to
    the verandah to catch the cool summer night's breeze?

now, now, now: ears make me a hearing organ as large as an
    elephant's and equally sharp
let me hear every syllable from this stranger's mouth; what will he
    say? for much, much, much, depends on what comes out of his
    mouth
the future of this house, all its joinery, all the principal members
from mother to me, depends on that answer

"damn it woman!" – eh, did i hear it right? the first profanity
   uttered in the famous house of laertes
utterances besides, from the lips of a stranger! if he's my father,
   then the rough sailor's
life has coarsened him; he needs civilizing
"damn it woman! who has ever moved my bed? who can move
   that bed i skilfully crafted from a single live olive bole?"

hip, hip, hip – hurray! hip, hip, hip – hurray! hip, hip, hip –
   hurray! father is back, hurray!
he needs not even add that to move that bed you have to cut down
   a live olive plant whose branches i have been pruning since i first
   saw them from down under
since i crawled under that bed and saw the green-starved little
   branches and yellowing leaves, gave them a tug and off they
   came; i have tended it ever since

these two know each other like your right hand whose fingers,
   when you interlace them with those of the left, dovetail, with the
   right thumb over the left; habitually
when all the tricks are over, there is yet that little detail left: like
   sikh fanatics who must wear the concealed small sword for the
   hara-kiri
as if the buckle with its hound-snared-fawn was not enough
   revelation, or the stringing of the massive bow and shooting
   through the twelve-skinned shield!

11

even before i was born, these two had been laying traps for
   catching interlopers; no wonder mother was circumspect
"be my wife and i shall build you a bed out of a live olive bole;
   then i shall cut down all the others and build our house over it"
what woman could be wooed thus and not accept the wager?
   besides, who in the whole wide world sleeps a herbal sleep in
   her house?

that bed i had shared with them in childhood; when duty called
   and he was at the front, i slept and wetted it till mother had a
   special cot made for me
in my childhood i must have smelt the changes of perfume from
   jasmine to musk when adults were making push-ups
those seemed like children's innocent games where one lies on
   her back and the other attempts to pump her, for fun, you
   understand?

now i understand it differently: conjugal life without push-ups
   is never amicable; between the chasing, catching, felling and
   smothering with kisses
the chemistry of love is generated; it is that which smoothes the
   life into which children are born and brought up
when we grow up, from toddling to adulthood, it is as a result of
   adult push-ups; hearty embraces keep the two together, are the
   house joinery

coda

yes, it was on that bed that i was engendered, that i was to be
   engendered, and much hung on the mystery of that live olive
   bole
now i, the silent witness of this scene, had better step forward and
   bring the two together; it is about time too that my presence is
   felt in my father's house:
"father odysseus, welcome to your home, to your wife, my dear
   mother, penelope!

"my dear mother, welcome to his home my dear father!
you two have lived apart for reasons beyond your control
the gods willed it, and some chapters had to run their course
some gods stood by you, strengthening your human resolve"

THAT ALONE
DESERVES
CELEBRATING

ii	telemachus' double takes an extended aegean
	rumination

1

here is he who seemed to know the detailed whereabouts of the
    family arsenal and how to command the servants masterfully
when he called me 'boy' i seemed to have heard 'son', if infant
    recollection can be believed:
there's that warmth and glow at heart you get when patted on the
    back, or backside, lovingly

had athena not told me who the stranger was… but i still need
    some more earthly revelations
for, with the grey-eyed lady who's made of myriad disguises, any
    semblance may be as real as unreal:
i will sit here where i am and like my mother watch and dismiss
    suitors, but remain circumspect

they say, my would-have-been age mate iphigenia the fated
    daughter of clytemnestra
had to die the death i should have undergone had my father not
    understood that sacrifices have substitutes
and that public morality, or what passes for it and becomes
    enshrined in tradition, was once an elders' edict

2

a king, that is an elevated man, decides to marry a girl engendered
   by a god in the guise of a goose, well, swan.
was it because he wanted to ask her how the egg grew, was
   hatched – inside or outside – the mother?
with a girl, leave alone human being, of such a mixed up
   parentage, should he not have left her alone?

my own mother, a kuku matron of birth, if she had noticed a
   child with deformities – elephant-like snout, completely white-
   coloured, handlelessness – she would have squashed it!
a prince with a prophecy came visiting, a prince from a feuding
   kingdom who'd been exiled because the seer had divined end of
   kingdom ahead,
divined he would bring the citadel down; but like all prophecies
   what looked impossible escaped the chop

blood, thou shalt not shed blood: even of a puking-mewling day-
   old child: deformed, incomplete, or evilly-destined
the nurse, the shepherd, the servant who was a house slave
   bought, or war captive or hunger-brought stranger, was always
   handed the child
destined to cause sufferings to parents, lineage, city, or allied
   kingdom – the tragic link

the child his lordly parents never squashed or smothered in
   swaddling clothes, left-handedly was exiled elsewhere
he returns home with somebody's wife, with his hostess, the wife
   to king menelaus the achaian host;
by now everyone seems to have forgotten or set aside the
   prophecy: paris would be the destruction of troy

3

with so many concubines around, couldn't menelaus have let his
    egg-wife go: she who hatches deaths?
when the thousand ships could not be launched the second time
    for lack of driving wind couldn't a return
– a return home – be ordered for the greek host? but the plot had
    to run its course, a cure for lack of wind: kill iphigenia.

who was this iphigenia but clytemnestra's first child? who called
    helen her half-aunt on the account –
on the account that after the god engendered helen from her
    mother, the mother was left for mortal men
and who would be the first all-human child, but clytemnestra,
    leda's daughter from tyndareus, wife of agamemnon, sacrificer
    of iphigenia

greek fates revolved around a few high profile families: oedipal;
    agamemnal, priamal or this one:
whenever they have appeared in the first generation, they must
    perforce plant the seeds for future complications and woes
agamemnon directs the foreign wars, brings to rubble priam's
    ancient citadel, only to come and die caught in a bath net

4

helen is famed for beauty that launched ten thousand ships, and
   all the forays, to-ings and fro-ings
clytemnestra stays at home, nurses a grudge, lodges a lover to help
   her lay the net into which ilion's destroyer –
ilion's destroyer will be hacked to pieces like a fish for sport and
   plaything in the hands of superman

clytemnestra, is that the coda to the trojan war? is it that after helen
   you've not heard something yet?
for, till i telemachus went to consult king menelaus and his errant
   wife helen, she had disappeared from the plot
and when i went to see her, she was all blaming the gods who
   caused her heart to waver and desert her man

why is this family so poetry-genic? i seem to have forgotten these
   two before me: and of odysseying and penelopeying
there were four or five heroes: agamemnon the king, achilles the
   master spearman, aeneas the trojan prince and –
and, lest you forget – odysseus my father: he whose world
   escapades rivalled the trojan war in greek popular belief

as for aeneas, the romans built an epic over his aeneiding from
   burning troy to relocate to seven-hilled rome
achillead could have been the other name for the iliad, only that
   the exploits in the field are credited to the c-in-c.
but the generals' wives left at home, penelope and clytemnestra,
   variously occupied their lives, or their lives were occupied for
   them

5

and there is a time for meting out the just deserts to the loafers at
   home who feast on the generals' wealth
clytemnestra got herself a man, her husband's sworn enemy who
   slept with the wife plotting her husband's demise;
penelope entertained the millionaires of ithaca, kept them
   distracted at arm's length, waiting, waiting

the iliad, people say, is a war poem: save for all those men falling
   down thunderously with their arms clattering over and about
   them
i swear i have a father who did not want to go to devise the deaths
   of so many people
and that man is my own father, odysseus, who was ready to feign
   madness if it could excuse him from war

for spring sowing, my father took his plough, prepared the land
   and sowed salt, white salt as seeds: to grow into what?
this i can remember vaguely, and it was confirmed by wet-nurse
   and shepherd, that i was laid by palamedes on the furlong
to trap my father the mad one: would he kill me in his madness, or
   would his shammed madness be unmasked?

6

mad agamemnon killed his own daughter to bribe the king of
wind to blow them to priam's citadel of ilion,
must wars be fought to their bitter ends? must kingly honour be
pursued till helen comes back to her first man?
couldn't king priam have told his fated child: let helen go so that
your prophecy is not fulfilled?

perhaps the stories were written after the events and we the artists
embellished them to our hearts' content? deciding the case in
retrospect:
perhaps the stories were fleshed up for each greek competition,
with each dramatist reconstructing the story lines, allocating
rights and wrongs according to changes in the moral outlook?
perhaps what is now true to life, all that is greek culture, history,
religious and moral philosophy, and knowledge are results of
seasonal cultural inundations compounding elaborations on
basic theses and precepts arising therefrom?

age mate, iphigenia, i sympathize with you: your life was clipped
off before your prime
history records your death as the single event that caused ilion to
fall: it brought on the wind that set the sails
then your chapter was neatly closed: mine had a comma, many
question marks, and now these open colons of ours:

childhood: how much of it did you have before your fame-hunting
father cut open your neck veins like a sacrificial goat?
childhood: did i even have one? with a mother forever touching up
her nose and meeting one suitor and his retinue after bath and
then another?
childhood: was there one to talk of, feasted on adventures and
escapades of parents/soldiers adventuring back from war?

7

iphigenia, clytemnestra's daughter, orestes' sister, you at least
   went to the front; if only to be slaughtered there
but i, penelope's son, nearly ploughed over in childhood and
   already salted for a feast, lived at home, a mother's appendage
and today, the war i had heard over and over from port to port, or
   from mouth to mouth, has come to face me at home

now that antinoos and the rest – all the who's who of ithacan
   society – have been slaughtered, including the mean and
   generous
now that their family members are carting them away for burial –
   or burning at the pyre – now: then what?
this slaughterer – winner and hero rolled into one – i now am sure
   will be declared my father and begin the fathering of me

the war ends, the master tactician turned trickster goes
   everywhere, world touring: what did he think of me? or my
   mother?
the war ends, why did he not send for me to share his experiences
   and learn his tricks of trade?
the war ends, a husband who had left his wife at home to fend for
   herself, leaves her to continue the usual game – was this a trick?

the war ends, mother receives stories from the rialto and wharfs,
   hearsays those sailors heard of his whereabouts,
did he not receive reciprocal stories from our own sailors about
   how things were going on at home?
if people reported about the carousing night after night, as well as
   gift giving, can the tongue-waggers be blamed?

8

the war ends, grandpa remains alive and a ruse for shroud-making
day after day, never mind the late nights' endings;
staying power, grandpa has in plenty, which happens to be this
family's special forte: to wait for signs
the war ends: wife waits for the husband, son for the father,
grandpa for son, nurse for thigh scar, and argus the dog for his
master

the war ends, a dog older than me recognizes his hunting
companion, yelps and dies: disappointed?
the war ends, unfaithful servants – and perhaps squealers too –
await dismissal or worse; the good ones await good old days
here again
the war ends, the wet-nurse of my father is still around to bathe
every family visitor, and at last spots the thigh scar!

the war ends, a dog older than me decides not to croak until a
particular stranger arrives
the war ends, the old shepherd remains alive, robust and
committed to the famous house;
the war ends, the wet-nurse of my father is still around, even after
tending my father, his memory and me

9

the dog yclept argus, the shepherd and this dog, joined by the wet-
nurse: they all wait, stay alive waiting, they say;
she who comes to me as in a dream, or in many disguises is a
goddess; they say she had no mother: both her father and mother
were zeus's mind:
the chief god conceived her and out of his mind, out of his head,
she emerged sans childhood, sans wet-nurse, sans milk teeth

athena of the dawn-grey eyes and divine skin, athena whose eyes
pierced you through since she x-rayed you;
athena, child of mind, conceived as an idea in the mind: the very
fruit of intellecting, patron saint of thought
athena, a goddess, but as capricious as any earthbound princess,
rivalling her brother apollo, was with me.

me, the boy whose childhood was lost since i was the last kid, and
had no elder sibling either,
when i looked into those dove-grey eyes, i stopped thinking and
let her words sink into my being,
if there was beauty, human body shaped, whose presence stopped
my breath, it was she, my athena, i was awash with you

10

in my youth we doubted the existence of gods and goddesses, but
    now i know that flawless being,
beauty that is perfection, does not come out of mortal fabrication,
    like the gods we create at the agora
and for now i wish to declare, if there are no goddesses, then i
    authorize athena to be my goddess

when, like a spy intelligence drop, she told me a certain stranger
    was coming my way, and that i should wait
wait for further instruction, then out of filial or amorous
    commitment to her, i was ready:
ready to go through hailstones or brimstones, to do her bidding
    whether father would return or not

these are the two parents i grew up with: the grey-eyed straight
    nose-bridged *mon amour* changeling
and the old soldier, nestor by name, who seemed to have known
    and brought up even my very father in his youth,
this one i accepted as my father, one generation past, who filled a
    boy's warm sense of fathering

11

now, to the task before us: these two have sat like that the whole
  evening: she awakened after the carnage;
he recovering his energy like an old man experiencing a teased
  orgasm after laying off for decades: the tedium is getting on my
  nerves; the shuttle moves but erratically
now: slow, lifeless, and as faulty as absentminded

i look at him and see him playing a strange chance game with an
  unseen opponent, sometimes he smiles
at other times he tightens his lips, has a grim visage and looks like
  an arm-twister now almost putting –
almost putting the other arm down, now almost losing the wager
  to see who is supreme in arm twisting

my mother's facial features are slackening, the shuttle moving
  slower, she yawns every now and then
normally by now she would be at her loom abandoning her last
  bath before retiring to bed
to go and undo the shroud-piece that she had worked so tirelessly
  diurnally: deconstructing

12

today is a night with a difference: suitors all dispatched to hades,
   their remains are being gathered up
today, the first death we saw was that of argus the dog that held
   the sky up so it did not crush us
after today, i fear grandpa will soon bid us adieu and prepare to
   go and join the godhead

the shroud that she could untie even in her sleep, it will not receive
   untying again
the woman, my mother will break the ice if she is the mother i
   have known these whole twenty years
in any case, she has to play the host: give a stranger from afar a
   place to lay down his tired bones

what was that i half-heard: a cough, my mother coughed as if to
   draw attention to her speech?
what was that she just said? did i hear it right? "odysseus, if your
   name is odysseus,
may i move your bed to the corridor where the wind blows? the
   weather is rather stifling inside there tonight."

13

now, she called him odysseus; now, she proceeded to ask him
  about his bed: would he want –
would he want it moved from its wonted place to the verandah
  where the breeze blows?
now, i wish i had more ears than two, more concentrated attention
  than one has in one life: that bed!

what will the stranger say? and let the cat out of the bag: that the
  bed be moved? that it is immobile?
as for me, i have never seen it moved and it seems to have one foot
  with twisted uppers but miracles do happen
the answer the stranger gives will clear all the doubts in my mind,
  as well as touch her heart

"damn it woman!" now here is a blaspheme i have never heard
  before in this house where there was no man!
"damn it woman! who has moved my bed, my bed made from a
  living olive bole? who could move it?"
father is back; he need not even have asked who could have
  moved it? it was immobile like a tree

coda

now i know: there are games spouses play, there are secrets one's
    parents share to which we are all strangers
and these two know one another like glove and hand: they are
    tight-fitting as the practised hands and gloves:
when all tricks are over, they know what last tests to give one
    another: especially my immobile mother

before i was even ever conceived, my father had already started
    making the snares that would enfamous him
to the spartan here, he had said: marry me and i shall build you a
    bed from a live olive bole and twist its branches
around it so i shall build the bedroom and then the whole house:
    no one but my father would have built a house that way

in my childhood i shared it with them: an innocent child who
    never knew i was in the way of conjugal bliss
when the market perfumes make way for the male musk, when
    speech is lost, replaced by grunts, another odour follows, then
    rest
in my childhood i thought push-ups were games children played
    for fun: or childhood aping adulthood

now i know that adult push-ups are the major components of
    married life: like the piercing glance,
the coy voice, the slight gesture as aspects of circumspection
as well as honouring the gods and tradition but going about it
    humanely.

iii   nights of pubescent telemachus

1

this is the time when she usually came, my fair, white-eyed athena
she'd come, like in a dream, like a swan landing with a flurry of
    feathers
then she would smother me with her wind, perfume, and that
    special bouquet:
being a goddess and feeding on the smell of burnt bull thigh bones
    wrapped in fat

fed furthermore on nectar which grows like manna from no
    earthly plant
after the long flight from mount olympus, she would glow and
    perfume my presence
the fumes from her armpits and those from the white area between
    her breasts
when she bends over me giving me a peep at her godly breasts
    and small nape hairs
these would be very unearthly, very heavenly and only a few
    mortals are privileged enough ...

now here she comes, dressed in the classical attic way, the style
    which beats beauty
very sparingly made: the dress hangs from the shoulders and
    flows down to the shanks
sometimes she wears a dress which looks so transparent to me i
    can see her breasts
and when she's so carried away emphasizing a point or urging me
    on, they would swell
and even heave with every breath: i would spare her the trouble of
    bursting by simply agreeing

2

at times without meaning to, my eyes would veer from breasts to
   belly then the mound of auburn hair between her legs
that triangular mound of kneadable hair invites aggression by the
   hand the way a cat or dog responds to caressing
when she'd sensed that i was fully magnetized by her static
   effulgent eyes and
as if she knew my next move would naturally have been to touch
   her, any part of her, she'd break the spell

and frustrate consummation of the telemachan complex:
the loving desire between a man and a goddess; perhaps one-sided
   love
the counterpart of the zeusian complex: god zeus pining for leda;
   and assuming any shape
and engendering helen for whose sake a thousand ships were
   launched
causing my father commandeered to go and devise the snares that
   finally brought ilion down, causing the odyssey and all that

(will there be a mortal girl to reap all these celestial desires?
am i to remain a lover of memories of pinnacles of love?
sometimes they call it platonic love; if i were you
i'd leave plato out of it, overburdened as he already is
by the memory of immortal socratic love)

book two:

trials and tribulations in the house
of atreus

I helen: the pregnant egg of menelaus

1

hated above all living things am i, helen of mycenae;
my name shall resound in the whole world as she who caused war
between my husband's people, and those of second-hated, paris
    alexandros

it is indisputable: a married man, a co-host of an honoured royal
    guest
one who knows the reciprocity between host and guest, would
    welcome and respect with good behaviour, a hostess left alone
such had the gods decreed, so that he who was arrested by
    darkness would sleep peacefully where his journey had been
    detained by night

but all of you who condemn me, look at my confusion: as my
    mother told my father and me when born
even zeus the god of all gods had fancied my mother, princess leda
    who loved to bathe where white swans romanced
"and one day he swam towards me on the shore; i thought it was a
    swan and felt mesmerized

"was it man, god, swan or a dream that parted my knees and
    planted the hateful seeds therein?
it is dishonourable to look a man in the face, engrossed in the
    throes of passion, as he pants and passes out
perhaps it was an earlier guest from the far east, tartarland or
    outer mongolia, or even eskimoland, who had done the hateful
    deed?"

nine months by-and-by, the water of life having hatched and
    matured came out puking
and mewling: it was helen making her first appearance unlike any
    mortal around
the wonder that i was set the world ashudder: only a god's child
    could i be or have been;

*

the oracles when consulted refused to elaborate, but confirmed the
common story: she the beautiful swan child is zeus' swan; still
impregnated

2

greeks, breeders of beauty, producers of masterpieces in stone, in
    words, make-believe; and the suppositions on the stage
came to observe this wonder, wished to possess it like a work of
    art to decorate their high-ceilinged visitor-welcoming halls
they swarmed into my father's palace, till my mother leda said
    "child, decide quickly, we cannot support this siege"

i had to call young sister clytemnestra: "come to my aid: those
    beauteous greek princes are all so godly, i can't choose;
some are tall and can see danger from afar, some so swift they'd
    win gold in any race, day or night; some spin wondrous tales
i wish i had days and nights, perhaps even a thousand nights if
    not more; some are still coming: how do i choose? give me the
    measure"

clytemnestra went playfully amongst these her brothers-in-law
    presumptive and using only the yardstick she had fashioned
eliminated the loud story makers, the wealthy who wore all their
    gold, and the ones who boasted ancestral exploits, including
    gods and goddesses as forebears
and came back with her mind made up: "there is one who uses
    measured words, is difficult to provoke, and overlooks little
    faults

"i would favour such: for guests you shall have, seeing you are far-
    famed and he is lordly, this is the son of atreus; not yet married.
this atreides, younger brother of agamemnon, host to all greek
    princes, i would that you consider him; with your playfulness he
    would treat you kindly
your younger sister clytemnestra would counsel you: end their
    sojourn away from home forthwith and let mama leda report to
    father"

the moment mama leda heard the choice she straightaway got up
    and spoke: "child how did you come to such mature decision?

i would have asked for more time and got confused: the gods are
    with you, these are wise aphrodite's words mastered into your
    heart:
your father, godly tyndareus, will be all magnanimity at receiving
    this choice: menelaus stands next to his brother agamemnon but
    is reputed the wiser and more valiant."

then it was that tyndareus summoned all suitors to divulge to
    them desirable helen's choice, how made and on whom it fell:
godly tyndareus, surrogate father of helen, notwithstanding his
    custodial role or because of it, first addressed himself to zeus,
then the gathered suitables, calling them all by name and their
    homes of abode, did not talk much: good news is better brief:

"all of you, young paragons, have favoured my palace with your
    visit: we have welcomed you; today your quest and guesthood
    ends;
our godly daughter, desirable helen, has passed her heavy-loaded
    decision to her mother, also deserved of our father zeus:
since only one husband she's allowed, like all mortals, she hopes
    you'll respect her choice; and good hunt for those we shall let
    return without a bride.

her choice is menelaus atreides"

3

before long, in order to make light the tedium, wise-speaking
   odysseus who also knows what passes through the hearts
   of men disappointed
got up and answered for his fellow suitors, he who could have
   won helen, but was impecunious and, goddess helen, she needed
   a palace and opulent life,
odysseus, who later married a stalwart-hearted wife, the
   circumspect penelope, princess of sparta, judiciously bred, thus
   spoke he:

"our father-in-law, we did not come to pressure, arm twist, sway
   the goddess helen with gifts, but to parade ourselves before her,
and, hoping aphrodite would guide her heart to give her the best
   man for her lord, protector and his master of her palace:
now that the lot has fallen on lordly menelaus, we wish him well,
   we congratulate you for earning so manly and godly a son-in-
   law

"now, my fellow suitors, the best man has won; let us compact
   ourselves by swearing the heavy oath:
should any suitor demean himself by challenging king menelaus
   over his luck we shall all come and fight against him
for helen will remain his wife, and his wife alone; i will come post-
   haste from famed ithaca, to make sure she remains as such"

the words were barely out before the suitors greeted them
   by hitting the sides of their shields with wooden sticks in
   agreement,
then a small contest was held to make them relax the muscles and
   ease the heavy heart of losers
those whose homes were near departed then and there; those from
   afar went home,
visiting fellow jilted suitors on their way, in friendship staying a
   day or more

4

the nuptials came and helen wended her way with menelaus to be
the queen of sparta and his wife
their happy marriage bed was graced with a baby daughter
hermione, a true chip from the atreides' line
but we shall deal with that when the time is ripe: it is not always
gods and goddesses or feuds that make us not toe the line of
culture

some subjects became unruly and menelaus had to leave his
honoured guest from troy alone with helen as tradition's hostess;
menelaus on his way, guest paris alexandros seduced the goddess
helen, honouring aphrodite's prize and dishonouring the nuptial
bed,
for which rudeness they fled to ilion, making menelaus veer off
course to report to big brother agamemnon

we next see helen on king priam's palace rampart, summoned to
show him the greek heroes and stalwarts:
the losing side's commander-in-chief sees his best men mowed
down by the greek war-machine, a sorry sight
and me helen, between tears and elation, telling my current father-
in-law which greek hero was pinning down which unfortunate
trojan whose luck had run out: a role no woman should ever
fall into

and when paris alexandros came to do battle one-on-one with the
cuckolded, valiant menelaus, he ran for his life from the field of
ares
straight to his high-vaulted bedroom royal to await aphrodite's
bringing of helen for love-making, both shamelessly
for once, the human nature of helen berated goddess aphrodite
who loved the trojans and paris, but did not support them in the
field as athena did her beloved achaians

but the two were magnetic in each other's company; berate paris
from afar, but when he's near, love-making takes over

perhaps swans in heat have so much load in their loins it must be
offloaded – that's the word – for ease and relaxation thereafter;
this, the last love paris would make, had better satisfy helen for,
poor girl, the end of their relationship is nigh

her return journey to face perhaps unspartan judgement is soon to
begin

the trojan horse, so-called, has been pushed inside the citadel;
  helen, knower of her former husband's people, knew what was
  inside this ruse
but helen, being paris's wife and troy's most treasured work of art,
  was guarded day and night
till she is recovered and troy razed to the ground, and its people
  and others taught a lesson: don't play with a civilization more
  advanced than your own

troy has fallen, menelaus is looking for his, shall we say, former
  wife? amongst all the waiting booty-women;
the wife of hector, judicious andromache, has been won by
  achilles' son neoptolemus, but what will happen to helen?
soon word goes out: report helen to menelaus, anyone who sees
  her, convey helen to menelaus

helen, on her knees, prays to aphrodite, fickle goddess who failed
  to defend her city of troy, aphrodite who'd bribed paris to name
  her fairest
and rewarded him with the most beautiful woman for a wife,
  had cheated athena and earned her wrath: the golden apple
  enamoured goddesses, she thought, with hera perhaps second;
her discord sown, she never fought for troy as much as cheated
  athena fought against it

menelaus finds helen on her knees, down on her luck; defenceless
  as a lizard, ready to receive her punishment:
manly menelaus' raises the golden sabre to sink it into her heart,
  finish with helen of the
thousand ship armada, fickle helen – plain slut – looks up and
  meets his eyes; was it prayer? was it in confession? begging for
  forgiveness? or was she leaving it to fate?

menelaus the man – humane man – saw in those eyes many
  messages, and reading their meanings confused him, as helen's
  choice of what next had been tough for her too;

menelaus – of all the big five: warrior achilles, kingly agamemnon,
   daring patroklos, thieving paris alexandros, hectoring hector –
   had a human end,
only humane menelaus and helen, humane odysseus and
   penelope, humane aeneas who lugged his blind father to become
   the icon of the new troy, rome

what shall we say? what shall we say? what shall we say?
shall we say there are moments in human life when a new message
   is brought into the world?
and neither bringer nor receiver
   knows what it is
nor the language of its decipherment?

going home, through thebes in egypt, helen and menelaus, in her
   or his way, set about their self-examination
helen seeing how fickle to go by a goddess's advice: was she –
   aphrodite – too old to make love to alexandros? frigid or what?
why was helen to be the one? why take helen so he'd release his
   sperm-filled sac from fear? was she a voyeur?

now beauty: why is beauty so hot that it sets on heat all who see it?
   why all the attention the choicest greek rulers and gentry paid,
who prayed and why for justice to be done, for his wife to be
   returned? was she the whitest child of a swan? or from some
   man close to the arctic circle?
or was the iliad the self-hating rage of brownish people to favour
   the fairest, the whitest in antiquity?

was it because the greek islands and isthmian formations were full
   of coloured people – including ethiopians, hence aesop – that a
   white person was a rarity and desired?
how come hector's white baby son had to be hurled to death? did
   the greeks think he would nurse revenge? were fair men planting
   fair children in greek women?
how come judicious andromache, the one trojan who always
   had wanted her, helen, released to the greeks, as should have
   been the case, survived, though as achilles' daughter-in-law,
   neoptolemos's concubine?

from all these indications it looks like odysseus who had not
   wanted to go to this war, is going to be spared death at sea,
and why not, for he has humane traits, has fashioned items to be
   identified by, measuring his human mind with foes who took as
   their measure the horse
and, though i and menelaus are still far from home, if a
   homecoming should come, i would detest further coaxing of
   aphrodite and henceforth remain human, all human

she turns to her sparer beside her, the man who did not do it
    as well as the interloper, who should not have been born, but
    whose humane parents had spared him,
this detestable paris who had to seek her out, like she was the key
    to civilizing troy so trojans would henceforth breed beautiful
    girls rather than breed horses for war
aristotle had preached that tension in tragedy needs to reach the
    mountain top to be released; is it ejaculation that is craved or the
    relaxation afterwards?

now, helen was one woman who couldn't be chopped into apple-
size presents to satisfy all suitors, so why desire her so, all you
humans going to war for her return?
was it helen, the museum piece who produced no child for troy
they were fighting for? or was it possession and loss?
most animals kill for food so why does man not eat human flesh
after the kill? have we lost the vital script?

this creation of gods and goddesses, spirits, heroes, kings and
queens, was it the real answer – interim perhaps – of some
sagacious poets,
to say only something higher than man can stand sentry against
animal man's inhuman acts against fellow humans? animals kill
animals for food, fair enough;
some men eat enemies, or any man they kill; others kill but show
respect to the dead in funerals; is that an interim morality?

perhaps clytemnestra was right, man had better die, and the gods
too, or first; and what her son orestes invented: man should
decide on any personal action to settle a score between equals, as
royalties in europe used to do
and not cause pain on the majority of mankind through needless
wars, and when man has done something, he should own up to
it, and when the consequence is bad,
should still accept the consequence, and suffer, if suffering is the
punishment

self-judgement chip implanted at birth or culturally inside one,
self-hell of guilt decreed by the sentry inside oneself that governs
one;
avoiding it, man should not buy favours from the so-called gods;
or hope to pile up salvation points in heaven,
or fear to do bad because of fear of second suffering in a spiritual
life when one is already devoid of senses and sensual organs, as
we know them!

*

do good. doing good is good

don't do bad because the bad is paining, hurting, is destructive,
the bad is ugly, is unseemly, is abominable, is unconscionable

the bad is bad.
full stop.

8

finally perhaps, after living with menelaus to exhaustion, i got
   bored with his love-making in the throes of passing sentence
   on some unfortunate culprit, and thought i deserved a youthful
   shaking up of things:
or with menelaus not giving me more children i had hoped a
   young love would give me some
alas, things were to remain the same; poor me!

as if preordained who had come along, but hungry paris
   alexandros! whilst it lasted we had fun, me and my alexandros;
   what aphrodite did with the apple though i don't know;
my alexandros, beloved of aphrodite, so wild and daring in the
   field of winning hearts, so adept at it, i'm sure i was not his first
he could have won me without urging from any goddess

he had his winning ways – ways that had stopped priam and
   hecuba from smothering him in the cradle
i am sure some men do better at winning human hearts than the
   gods and goddesses, and it is up to you to imagine what goddess
   he might have had!
and also human beings! frail queens and haggard kings in their
   various greek palaces must have envied me for this: but who
   cares, the deed is done, the just deserts meted out: troy is no
   more, and i am here

ancient as these neglected women are, if i were not returned to
   marriage bondage who knows how many other old women
   would have eloped with younger princes;
they plotted together, gathered all their children, shepherds, farm
   hands, slaves and went to agamemnon to get me back; especially
   those i had jilted were loud in denunciation
they envied me my second marriage these sour grapes of flat lands
   and foaming coasts, they came to destroy me and the more royal
   life i enjoyed

they razed troy to the ground, as if the stone-constructions had
    taken me to troy, and ten years they were at it
the trojans shored up their manhood for ten years; the achaians
    took ten years to come to the climax: two prize bulls working up
    a concerted orgasm for ten years!
had the trojans stood their ground for one more year, perhaps the
    mission would have been abandoned

if at the end of the iliad, paris had been left alive and i had
    remained in troy, where, ask the critics at the agora, has poetic
    justice gone?
and which playwright would have won the kudos of that year? it
    was for the sake of poetic justice that paris perished in troy
and i had to be dragged back to sparta to live my last years with
    memories, a long sterile life amid jeers from my queenly sisters-
    in-law

as for menelaus, he wears his kingly heart at home and in the
    office, so dutiful, he has no time for anything else;
as they say in papua new guinea pidgin: *dat is samting blong
    em*; i am on my way back to mycenae with my legal husband
    menelaus to the humdrum of married life;
i should have died with paris, my paris, and remained as ashes in
    troy

coda

as for troy, i left nothing in troy
who knows if troy was not a bogey to deter future helens
from leaving their menelauses?

II   cassandra: the unbelievable prophet of apollo

i   *outside the gate of troy*

1

cassandra is my name, and my father is priam, king of troy
i am human but divinely beautiful by any god's standard;
so beautiful, lord apollo approached me for dalliance, god though
   he is.

one brother of mine is alexandros, better known as paris;
he against whom at birth the oracles had opined utter destruction
   of the citadel of troy, but his parents, my mum and dad, ignored
   them,
paris brought down our proud mountain lookout, brought ruin to
   the kingdom

lord-king-apollo chose me for his own; he being a god i knew we'd
   never cohabit, live together as husband and wife, be part of each
   other's family, socialize;
though he tempted me with the gift of prophecy he could do the
   deed in any guise, even left me with child
but seeing i was loath, and that he couldn't gainsay the gift, i was
   cursed with not being believed

looking back, though, unbelief didn't start with me: the prophecy
   said paris was to be smothered
but our mother queen hecuba, and priam our father the king, were
   human enough to give him to the shepherds
second midwife and nurse that they were: 'never kill' is their vow
   to goddess artemis of births; half-suspecting the worst, but not
   by them, they did a left-handed deed

the worst events-before-they-happened, i see, designed deeds
   approaching before they strike, so rail as i might, people turn
   deaf ears like choruses in our plays:

they hear but are deaf to my prognostications; i am prometheus
  for nothing; better i were an epimetheus uselessly wringing his
  hands outside the murder room
apollo, peevish that he is, what use designating him a god? some
  humans see and do better than this lady dramatist

2

troy, troy, troy: my beautiful city troy: only a few days are you left
    – left to stand: in precisely four days, troy, our troy, shall stand
    no more,
father priam will crumble with his citadel, i shall be dragged as
    booty, andromache's only child astyanax shall be hurled to his
    death:
why let live the possible avenger? though aeneas will trudge away
    piggybacking his blind father anchises

these things shall come to pass: ten years of siege are no joke:
    when odysseus the persistent has set his heart to it:
he who nestles up a hill has no escape, the encirclers down below
    will get him, by and by
birds nestle there and take to flight when endangered but son of
    man is clueless: even castles succumb to flying rockets

all i see is no life in ilion; perhaps aeneas's project of flight to move
    troy to rome will create a greater troy protected by many a god
    and goddess
unencumbered with curses and ancestral feuds, blind-father-
    carrier will stagger with his engenderer burden from troy to
    future troy and plant a seven-hilled new city
the gods abhor unalloyed success: let achaians destroy troy but
    aeneas will raise up rome, grander than ilion, or mycenae

as for the house of priam, we shall feature as supporting casts in
    greek heroic tragedies and poems: trojans playing the losers,
gloating greeks shall have achilles as *primus inter pares*, second-
    fiddled by hector; agamemnon shadowed by priam,
andromache, great hector's wife, as a booty wife to neoptolemus
    after hector's son is flung to death

and here i am waiting to be wived by agamemnon, victorious king
    of athens: god apollo's approaches i could rebuff but atreides'
    son i dare not spurn

perhaps wise adviser andromache who, not unlike me, was also
  unbelieved by her lord hector
shall live as wife to another achaian
dead me, i shall join these sprinters in hades: achilles' company

paris, patroklos, hector, heroes destined to die young: murderers
  that they are, they shall compare notes of plans and rebuffs,
  regrets and lies, all useless
nobody is going to take a true account of what was or was not said
  under the earth! poets and prophets only surmise:
if only it were possible for the dead to come back and
  communicate their thoughts to their dear ones still living on
  earth!

3

burn, burn, burn troy burn; burn, burn, burn ilion burn: you were
   destined to burn for achaians, being flat seaside folk, envied your
   citadel perch
the fortune-tellers had foreseen this day when they had read paris'
   oracles aright, but even messages from gods, in the minds of
   men and women, remain undone
burn, burn, burn troy burn: we humans are actors in the plays of
   gods – gods whose joint masters over us are the fates; perhaps
   only overshadowed by fate itself

a tragic play is crafted, a scene is selected, characters are assigned
   roles: the plot unfolds, the reel rolls, the script plays itself out,
this is a play where the humans are powerless; when the gods
   run out of ideas, like our playwrights, out of the machine, they
   physically descend to the stage
pushing things to a tragic end; playwright gods do not seamlessly
   tailor the plot: when stuck for a way forward they appear
   onstage

there was never a troy, except the morality play as vehicle for
   religious warnings dutifully chorused
a heroic age ends in the deaths of heroes, some in battle, some in
   bathtubs, a few out of old age, or natural deaths
and those the new gods love survive to draw a moral: half human,
   half-goddess helen lives twice with husband menelaus

since i am a seer, prophet unbelieved, what do i care if i spill all i
   see?
seeing eye, seeing too clearly the murky today, sees a horrifically
   red future:
sees, with the groaning cries in hades the results of prophecies
   unbelieved

there are no gods but prescient religious poets' lessons to mankind
   seen in the dark;
in the chilly desert night sky, lying on their backs, observing the
   cosmos, they see –

they see clearly what the dwellers in the valleys snoring after a
   heavy vegetable meal do not see

one conclusion they all draw: man is too arrogant and
   experimental if not hampered;
what then is strong enough to keep him on a straight and narrow
   path but hope of a bespoken and sworn afterlife where justice
   dwells? the straight-pathers separated from their crooked many
   tormentors?
so opined the few ancient god-creators

4

what do these people see; my fellow eternal seers? they see
    inquisitive mankind hurtling down a maelstrom, but even when
    warned by the far-seeing ones man the doubter follows the
    bellwether to slaughtery
man, prescient man, experimental man, daredevil man, who as a
    child tears off grasshoppers' legs and wings, does he care how
    others feel? his pound of flesh he'll demand even from inside the
    breast-covered chest, though the debtor and the owed perish in
    the pursuit
man makes toy-work of his fellow man for his entertainment:
    it has had its day; the once-a-millennium philosophical
    poets designed a way out with gods, satans and their human
    surrogates

the only way out, the seers up the olympuses, mount aboras,
    kilimanjaros, ararats, hiroshimas, have one word: religion
create a myth stronger than truth; create mental realities stronger
    than earthly realities; stronger than men and women can pull
    apart
create a work of fiction imbued with greater believability, so that
    men, in their dreams, see them as realer than real, works defying
    the realists and the imaginists

some of these poems have gods, have goddesses, princessly gods,
    princely goddesses, with angels and earthly kings who act as
    standby gods;
only fate defeats them; most god-creators end up leaving neither
    god nor devil in sole control of the whole creation or ownership
    of overall power
the orchestration proceeds from power or overlordship, to fate, or
    fortune

some are so powerful, these gods, they live lonely lives, but crave
    human company, jealously guarding against interlopers and
    dethroners; some so jealous they can destroy a million nonlovers
    or followers of competing god-creators

some are not so powerful though they live above earth, addresses
   unknown, and leave undestroyed rival gods behind to tempt
   humans who are still alive to meticulously walk the narrow
   straight path and guard against straying to the devil's land
failures will end up not occupying the grand position reserved for
   the upright; so a virtual world is created with avenues and gps,
   the fire down under so real and so embellished by latter-day
   poet-prophets; what do they know of the real good world?

how do they know more about the stygian or some elysian world?
   i cassandra, knowing well the dark deeds of mankind, look back
   and forth and have decided
which is better: a religion-less world, or an alternative world
   religion reformed from those around so that limits are set
   against man's fecund experimentation in this world dark and
   deep

ii.   outside the lion gate of mycenae

5

now we're outside this lion gate of mycenae, wrenched from a
    citadel elsewhere, from a city worse done by than my hymenal
    citadel of troy
it is full of discord and smells of – and i smell my blood, my
    spilled blood, it tickles my nose and i see it in the bathtub; i am
    being hatched already: take me out of here!
my man, agamemnon, so strong against us in troy has gone to
    hades already: some heroes! take me out of here!

but we are still outside the gate; the throng is great; these stayers at
    home never sent other soldiers to the front, for ten years
they have come to welcome their world-beating agamemnon
    atreides; some are apprehensive, the queen has a lover, a cousin-
    in-law
they have come in a solid blind body, victorious mycenae agloat;
    now troy lives no more, but dissension has come; the enemies at
    home are waiting

one person is awaited, for the next step forward; aegisthus is still
    a long way off, aegisthus, the son of cheated pretender king
    pelops, produced by pelops' son out of his own daughter in
    exile,
and clytemnestra has halted proceedings till he comes; then her
    dirty plot can work, the net is ready, the bath newly painted
    white; the clear white water is waiting
so here i wait, with my knowledge inside me, knowledge of what
    is in store for me too, being tantalizingly near

now, there is a stir on the western side, on the left side, the left-
    handed action is near: the queen's emissary had adumbrated his
    tale of our approach
for co-conspirator aegisthus, a cousin of agamemnon with whom
    a blood feud exists, who needed no urging for his plot within a
    plot

he's been roped into action – clytemnestra thought she was urging
    a stranger – but he's saving himself; let her plan succeed, he'll be
    a mere accomplice, but most beneficial

now the lion-gated citadel has its doors flung wide open; we're
    welcomed by the regicides; choruses and a whole lot of
    onlookers
soon he'll be ushered to his room, my master-to-be atreides,
    undressed and led to the bathroom to be hacked and dispatched
    to where all the dead go
and my fate, the footnote to their trojan victory shall take place!
    adieu, life adieu; adieu and good luck to aeneas and his cargo; to
    andromache, and my father priam and mother hecuba

i am on my way to reunite with you tonight

III   agamemnon: the sacker of troy dies in a mycenaean bathtub

1

my name is agamemnon, otherwise called atreides on grounds of
    parenthood; king of mycenae am i, menelaus is of sparta
we both issued from resourceful atreus's loins, of the famous fated
    line: the doomed house of atreus
it was because of helen, menelaus' wayward wife who eloped with
    paris, that we went to war in far-away ilion, unscalable ilion

there are many stories attached to us as there are to other great
    houses; just think of oedipus
and you realize that when oracles at birth are unpropitious they
    will still act themselves out
so are those attached to the houses of priam, midas, pelops,
    achilles' father, and our house of atreus

they say our sire once had a dispute with his brother, for the
    throne of mycenae and goddess athena told dad to wager with
    uncle over an east-setting sun
if that took place uncle would surrender his claim to kingship:
    if not, dad would lose; the gods prefer some mortals to others;
    pelops thought zeus was even-handed
but for once he set the sun in the east! and uncle had fallen into
    the god's machination; did a brighter-than-the-sun meteor streak
    eastward after sunset?

and he, pelops, later avenged himself by making grandma his
    lover in secret: climbing on the throne, as it were; enraged
    granddad organized a feast and cooked uncle's sons for him to
    devour; unsuspecting as ever!
one of our cousins who was not fed to uncle survived to later
    continue the feud; he never went with us to troy, and seemed
    never to have favoured helen with suit, when all greece had
    lined up wagering preference

it was reported to me in my absence at the trojan front, he had teamed up with clytemnestra; are they rehearsing a revenge, or is this encirclement of me in the bathtub for real? she recruited him to murder us! the net is closing now

2

at the front, the wind stood obdurately still and the army and
    allies were twitchy with boredom
especially when the snake foretold emerged from a hole and killed
    the nine small birds
and calchas interpreted that we would encamp nine years outside
    troy, windless, for we had to placate snake-footed typhon

begetter of wind, god typhon had a grudge against us and would
    take no substitution, however much we urged
except the blood of my daughter iphigeneia, shed by my own
    hand, which any true human parent would resent, or not do
    light-heartedly
but uneasy rests the crown on his head, leader of others' kids to
    war; the gods must know if you have it in you to sacrifice: shed
    your own blood first

the god-given test was he who dares lead others' children to death
    for the sake of his glory at war
had better swallow the bitter taste of his daughter's red salty blood
    spilled by himself, no less
i had to show that this was a price i would pay for history's sake;
    my sister-in-law was abducted, my brother king came to me for
    help: what could i do?

i held her neck up, calchas or another held her body, and with my
    right hand i gashed her throat; my red blood in her veins gushed
    out, i couldn't stand it
i went and retched, threw up this left-handed act of placating
    typhon; i hope he enjoyed it!
now the accursed deed was done, we looked forward to going
    to troy; i had proved myself a leader of men into daring deeds,
    killing deeds!

we had her, my daughter, put to death, a left-handed deed, tore
    her throat, but it assured them all, challenged by uppity trojans,
    uppity paris the traitor-visitor,

that i had what it takes in this war of cultured achaia and the
  uncivilized refractory trojans
with that done, the confederation was strengthened; it stood
  strong even when achilles
sulked; nine years waiting for obviation of supremacy of his spear,
  they couldn't go back empty-handed

little did i suspect that wife clytemnestra would bear me such a
  grudge for a manly act in the field of war; what do women and
  loafers at home know of the neck-clamps in war?
she, perhaps resenting sister helen's fame, wanted to carve for
  herself a role; and has found a small niche to be painted into, and
  what a niche! for crying out loud!
she teamed up with feuding aegisthus to await my return and
  smother me in the bath! for her, killing the defeater of trojans
  was greater glory, however treacherous

3

short of marrying our sisters and cousins, when we marry people
  from outside who do not have the grudge of feud in their blood
  we court disaster too
they cannot sympathize with a feud in the livery of an ancestral
  name and palace-tied lands
they may not even synthetize with the heavy crown we wear, or
  the *noblesse* and *oblige* that crowned heads bear

the houses they came from are parvenu, she takes wealth at face
  value: death of the daughter as a tool, equals that of a king; she,
  not born of a swan, envied her sister and identified more with
  human children
knew not how her own father bore the cuckolding and accepted
  the swan camouflage, or is it our special relationship with the
  gods that casts us apart from the uncomprehending hoi polloi?
are there heads so thick, they are not penetrable by religious
  preachings and acted scenes at the agora? or is it that religion is
  losing its hold on people, so the greeks are becoming profane?

religious acts became pageantries and tragedies, deteriorated to
  comedies, and later farces
what with socrates gladly swallowing the hemlock for the charges
  of heresy against the olympian gods?
perhaps clytemnestra does not believe in human interference
  in the movements of the winds? human propitiation of
  departmental gods to do their divine duty?

why did she not wait till i returned, then quiz me about the
  'murder' as she called it, of her daughter? why did not the gods
  send their emissaries to brief her?
for zeus' sake iphigenia is from my loins too, and i, not light-
  heartedly, account for the life of every achaian soldier lost, for
  the trojans we killed
it was the thing to do: confirm belief in oracles; she's not even
  grateful for my rescuing and returning to her palace her
  wayward sister helen

the deed was done: the most powerful man of the trojan war was
   caught naked in a net and killed, his blood reddening the clean
   white water
i, who had commanded a thousand ships, killed by my wife and
   cousin; a commander-in-chief disarmed and drowned in his own
   family bathtub, like a drugged rat or cat
while washing off the soil of troy and relaxing tired muscles after
   the long journey home and nine years of war

that any living person should not count himself lucky, i now
   believe i used to doubt its truth
poets are also prophets: they lay traps for strangers in the
   truthworld
the real truthworld is the world of the dead reports from the
   netherlands of the danes, swiss, inuits or grandparents long
   before death testifies to their existences

4

and, now, in this underworld where i am mixed with all who
    died before or after the war i am being shaken in my faith in the
    achaian gods
power is a relative thing: you have it at the front; demobbed you
    join the commoners, become a peasant, perhaps respected by
    your wife if you are lucky
and with power left outside the bath, you enter the water in your
    birthday suit and the tub is your grave?

there is a general will, which is greater than a person's individual
    will
a group with a group will and agenda, when they are bound
    together, are a force
when god pan is with them and they rush like a herd of bison
    from the cold winter snow all of one mind, hurtling down cliffs,
    if heading that way

and maybe a crowned head needs to keep abreast of current events
    by every night reviewing official decisions against popular view
    and opposition opinions
and the feudal agenda they wield; hector with an andromache,
    or better still a nestor, would debate the individual agenda and
    decision for each day
or review the day's occurrences, something we did not do, big
    population number hunters that we were

the playwrights, maybe, were right: iphigenia did not deserve
    to die; was there no deer to substitute for her? latter-day
    playwrights tried to save my individual guilt
or will try, in seasons to come; hosts tried to assuage my spiritual
    wound by laughing it off but i have remorse too, not for
    clytemnestra's reasons
homer is right: i killed our daughter with my hands, so let my
    human guilt sink deeper; group thought is blinding but where to
    get power over crowds without making sacrifices?

this deed that i committed, jewish playwrights dodged it for
   abraham, isaac was saved, a thicket-caught ram replaced the
   human sacrifice
even yahweh, god of the jews, craved human blood till symbolism
   won over realism, so let a sheep or deer take over, replace the
   human blood
then how come mary's son is sacrificed after isaac had been
   spared? did the sun really not rise this time from the west?

latterday poets and moral reformists, to spare the evildoer social
   sanction, invented the substitute animal sacrifice to donate the
   all-important blood
between the sophists and his sophistry and the sacrifices and his
   blood substitute the difference is the same: they are both face-
   savers
iphigenia my love i shall look you up before earthtime sunset and
   say i am sorry and have paid for it

truth of religion or eternals conveyed through symbols and
   symbolisms
are one notch above realism but a long and crooked notch
   that be
inside and outside of the entanglement, without understanding
   what the *it* was or was about

5

in any case, why do greek gods who feed on ambrosia and inhale
the smell of burning fat-wrapped thighbone need the flesh of
man or sheep, toothless that they are?
what is this need for human blood? or teeth? ambrosia cannot be
chewed: it is drunk; for the smell of burning fat you need large
nostrils
it is humans whose readiness is tested; he who would kill his own
child is ready for greater 'sin'? the meat of the sacrificial sheep is
there for officiants and attendants to eat

deeds of sacrifice and deeds of bloodletting: crossing the ethical
rubicon, is the tested readiness and appropriateness
and it is religious reform if you say: use an entangled ram to
save your son who is too big; is that enough to shrive the guilt?
there's no more to it?
and who are you saving but the sacrificers: abraham sparing isaac
is a moral coward delivered from the dead weight of guilt

he can bear the sign of cain without the name of fratricide
attached, for whoever sins when he cuts the throat of the
innocent sheep is shrived
it is bordering on sacrilege when humans, the heroic sacrifice-
bearing men, no longer commit murder, but do what later greeks
did:
sacrificed the knife that did the slaughter by hurling it to the sea: it
killed the sheep dead, therefore had to die, we shall eat the ram
and drown our tears in wine.

had we been so lax as to replace my iphigenia with a deer, would i
have done it – accepted the deer artemis offered – as our secret?
had i sunk to such a depth, would i have returned home a hero
to that city-full welcome? for myself, for age, i did what was
royally, morally and politically correct, and authorized
this revisionism is a new trend: how do we judge the deeds of a
thousand years ago? and think we can rewrite the rationale for
the trojan war and all its deeds?

*

our past is but a prologue to your present impasse: face your own
  demeanour squarely

IV clytemnestra: the stay-at-home housewife who kills the great general

1

they call me clytemnestra, they who know me, know i am human
and have feelings but am overshadowed by older sister helen
unlike helen, hatched from an egg, swan-fertilized by zeus' loins, i
do not care for that rigmarole:
i am human, all human, from tyndareus who fathered me on
leda's bosom, he a man, she his married wife

in my father's house there is no feudal curse, or cannibalism, or
incest; how zeus came in like a swan is something else
it was my mother's favouring of a spot on the river bend
frequented by a swan that made the story plausible.
and zeus, they say, found it easy to mix with birds and humans,
and the story was easily believed, this yarn of leda raped by a
swan

why a god, zeus himself, should fancy human beauty and
unlawfully rape her, mischievously putting it out that he entered
her in the form of a swan
can only be left to the gods of earlier races to mull over, for chiefs
and gods are so imperious or their names are used for iniquitous
human deeds
don't they have goddesses to dilly-dally with rather than sully
human life with strange creations; why not beauteous instead of
duteous?

now, one would have thought the gods' appearances were for the
good of mankind, but don't deceive yourself, or be deceived
the deeds that are laid at the gods' feet, come on! wake up! some
are worse than ordinary men or women do
so when chiefs defile others' wives or daughters, they give it out
that the gods are to blame: poor humans, is man so gullibly
born?

so, my mother, perhaps with a white-skinned foreign visitor,
hence a new breed of looks, did a dark deed and produced a fair
beauty, beautiful beyond all local ken
and the passing visitor, here nine months earlier, was thus turned
into a swan, the swan of zeus!
a swan to hump my mother? beautiful women are so fertile in
covering up, especially dark deeds of a sexual nature when
explaining wrongs against spouses; helen will say the gods made
her couple with paris! and menelaus will believe her!

2

so, helen was born, this mixed-breed beauty, perhaps mongolian,
   from tartarland or beyond caucasus-loins conceived? or even
   eskimoid or chinoid?
if so i would not blame her, for such occasions streak into view
   once in a thousand years, like sleeping with a martian!
helen is the belle beyond all belles: all peloponnesians were agog
   at her sight; not even zeus could claim her parenting!

all men: kings, princes, heroes presented their visiting cards but
   only menelaus, the weakling, was favoured
no wonder odysseus, foreseeing problems from future passing
   visitors, bonded every suitor to menelaus' defence
protecting from their spermatozoa this nefertiti with that stately
   neck and poise of the egyptian queen to come, was an affair of
   state

for her it was hard, too, picking the right card: the qualities that
   would let her rule over him
and elder sister turned to me, just a human, for an assist; i said...:
   "sis, take it easy: who worships you?
take him who will lick wine from your feet, not the fighting heroes
   or crowned kings, not even people of wealth, for they are proud,
   with reason"

that's how menelaus was picked, a man too trusting for his own
   good; she heated the loins of all the peloponnese
and even paris, son of priam was alerted; after cuckolding
   menelaus he would return to lick wine from her toes
he, who had a story to tell, came sniffing and, being the male-
   factor of her beauty, was a match, so where did she lick her
   wine? ask any mario!

menelaus, worshipper of the swan egg story, went royally to visit
   all over spartaland and his wife

who was not so spartan with romance, took off with paris – paris
who aspired to transplant greek civilization to asia minor; as she
had conquered the aegean sea,
she went to lay all troy low; how could asia let this chance pass
by? breeders of horses versus breeders of beauty?

and the rest is history; the aim they said was to rescue helen,
uphold the fame of the achaians or, they said, to civilize troy so
asia minor wouldn't be left behind
"dare take one wife from us," said side a, "and we shall come and
reduce your city to ashes."
said side b, "that will be no cakewalk," and it was done; but at a
price; civilization-teaching helen, taken to rome, would produce
a grander athens

3

didn't leda have other girls? are we all eclipsed by helen of swan-
egg fame? these thoughts were visiting me every night
now i was left at home, and my daughter duped to go to the front:
and for what? to appease artemis
to be killed, to have life squashed out of her; to be drowned in the
sea to assuage artemis' spite?

and agamemnon does it as if he knows how to get pregnant, spit
the early pregnancy spit, inflated for nine months, knows how to
keep a foetus
or how to nurse a foreign body in one's womb, to give a child
milk, to have it shit and puke on you, to nurse in fever or
dysentery day and night
did agamemnon own iphigenia to summon her and murder her as
he pleased? was it for glory or fame? his fame and greek glory?
men!

did i, clytemnestra, not have a say? the soothsayer calchas said the
wind would only come when my daughter's blood was spilled in
the aegean sea
umuofia people would have used a slave girl, slain by another
man than their chief; the wind would have blown on the western
hillside some year and repeat
would it not change and blow to troy when the second or third
season came? these men pining for wives and feasts at home, did
they know what awaited them?

i, a human, have been keeping a record of the winds and am
amazed; as promptly as the seasons change, so do the directions
of the wind
calchas be damned! or is it that soldiers got bored of hanging
around doing nothing when they were meant to go to troy?
don't con me with your false religions, shedding the blood of
others; the aegean sea is too large to feel the effect of my small
daughter's blood

as far as i am concerned – concerned and keeping records of the
winds – i am aghast
i had thought my husband wiser than his brother, or father-in-law
or our father, but in matters of state
he was duped to commit murder; in matters of love men accept
cover-ups, especially war tacticians adept in martian battles and
inept at home

4

well, hubby agamemnon, i hope you've enjoyed your honeymoon
    whilst on the charted ripply route with your far-seeing bride,
winner of the war of two worlds, achaia and ilion, i am more than
    ready for a contest; i and your cousin aegisthus have a strange
    welcome for cassandra and you
within a few hours hades will have two newcomers, a former king
    and his concubine, the fortune reader screaming to deaf-ears

inbreeding is the order of things in your royal households, i now
    surmise
for where else can a prince romp free except with sisters, cousins
    and sisters-in-law?
where else should a prince from another land romp free except in
    another palace?

so, zeus, or whoever it was who planted seed in my mother
    enjoyed his stay and dalliance; so, paris, comes visiting and his
    host goes inspecting his far-flung domains
so, in exile, pelops finds his daughter and rapes her, of all people,
    and other deeds were secretly done, some secretly undone:
he who lay with his cousin-brother's wife, in revenge, they say;
    only helen knows the count

agamemnon, atreus' son, we here have an incestuous son,
    pelopia's child fathered by her father, thystes, a name you'd
    remember in your feuding history
first cousin of yours, who knows how his line lost the claim to the
    throne of mycenae, is my accomplice:
between us we have hatched your murder and cassandra's, a
    conscious deed; no god or mortal ordered us, we did it from our
    free will: elderly women crave youthful shake ups!

agamemnon *mon amour*, with heavy heart i shall smother you in
    the bathtub with manly assistance from aegisthus,

who also has his feudal grudge against your line, besides his blood
   is hot! and what a lover he is!
i bring to conclusion the trojan war, now that i have a footnote of
   note in it!

5

now the deed is done, i can breathe easy; iphigenia your death is
   avenged, you whose budding future life was smothered
by a father's war-roughened hands, i have this day made him pay
   for it, witnessed by cassandra.
wherever your remains may lie, may they rest in peace

i am left with two more children: orestes and electra, who should
   be around somewhere, too young to understand today's
   avenging deed, especially infant orestes:
the wild card is electra: but we shall deal with them by and by,
   once you have killed, the next kill demands no heart search,
for the last-killed demands you dispatch another to follow, for
   reassurance that his killer was no weakling

for me now, the priests and their shrines, soothsayers and their
   prophecies, are things of doubt, relics of the past: we now live in
   the new world of research and science,
proof, and preparations to meet eventualities are what guide us;
   now that my husband (the late) has forced me to do so easily
   what took troy so long *not* to achieve
i shall deal with everything come what may: if electra wants war
   we shall fight

in preparation for future eventualities, i shall keep the throne of
   mycenae;
aegisthus fits into this palace which, but for zeus, could have been
   his, and he will be my consort, after all
agamemnon can enjoy his bride in the nether world and we shall
   do it here, anywhere the hunger catches us

why should i suffer an empty bed, cold nights, silent darkness and
   loneliness as if there were no spare husbands around? fit and
   energetic too. my mario!
religion is receiving a rethink at our hands; the dead now in the
   west should have soulmates down there too; may they have
   orgasms!

mankind has too long refrained from acknowledging its guilt and
blamed things on the gods; aegisthus, come, let's make love
while we still may

if you want life better lived then better it here; improve it with
human senses and for the senses and the humans here
if wishes were horses, beggars would ride; between man and
mountain it is man who goes to the mountain
don't science-fictionalize life and then believe in the creation of
your mind born of fears of the enormities man and earth have
created between themselves

confront reality like clytemnestra

V   orestes:

i   the prince who defeated the goddesses

1

i am known as orestes, youngest child of my father, the murdered
    king agamemnon
i was but an infant when she who gave birth to me conspired with
    her cousin-in-law aegisthus to murder my father the king just
    back from troy
but sister electra spirited me off to king strophius' palace in phocis

there i grew up, well protected from those who wished to end our
    line, including suspected me
and when i came of age my protector, god apollo, called me to do
    the honoured job, deal with clytemnestra and aegisthus;
and avenge my father's murder, get back the kingship that was
    mine, to end the inter-familial feud

and to requite cassandra, his recipient of divine power: prophecy
    (behaving like the jilted suitor, still loving his first love)
all this was told me by the god who cared for me and his mission
    was dear to his heart
and because sister electra wanted it, as did all mycenae; the time
    was ripe

i had another big sister, fated iphigenia, who had to die so the
    wind would blow to fated troy
the wind to blow the death-dispatching achaians to erase from the
    face of mother earth the hitherto unassailable ilion
and bring back helen, errant wife of uncle menelaus, and my
    mother's sister

iphigenia was slaughtered on the altar of contention between king
    agamemnon and queen clytemnestra

but the queen, with daughter's blood shed (daughter to
agamemnon too), thirsted for more blood, more royal blood, to
get her a mention in the annals of history:
killer of the destroyer of troy was queen clytemnestra, his royal
consort

had the loss been sister iphigenia alone, perhaps the world would
     have settled for the charge against agamemnon
but mother's cousin-in-law was already sharing bed and crown
     with her and keeping my inheritance from me when i was old
     enough to rule my father's ancestral domain

they were already one when father was at war, but the day
     agamemnon was arriving aegisthus kept away
and showed up for the great reception, following his cousin closely
     to the bath for the murder
and when agamemnon was undressed and quite unarmed they
     threw the net around him and drowned life out of him

they made short work of killing cassandra, who had seen it
     coming, but was unbelieved in mycenae as in troy
the duo's victory speech was prepared but no one wished to hear
     it; they all ran home
and judicious electra spirited me away to a faithful friend of my
     father's, where i was well preserved

until she and apollo would spur me to put an end to usurpers and
     usurpation –
usurpation by regicide, let us call it by its legal name, remove it
     from neuter and unsinfulness
i am on my way to do the deed, accompanied by the king's son, a
     companion, unveering cousin pylades

we went, found flabby-girthed aegisthus relaxing on a settee, quite
     unarmed, like my father of old, not expecting my return
and helped by beloved pylades, my sword found its way right to
     the heart
and mother, recognising me, sought in vain to exert maternal
     power begging for forgiveness: she too we sent to hades

          *

revenge time is no time for forgiveness

what should follow but the revenge of the furies for matricide; one
　　god demands a deed, another castigates the same
where the furies were when the king was killed baffles me still,
　　but i was harassed to distraction by them
moving from shrine to shrine, seeking respite and rest of mind,
　　without apollo's succour

pushed to madness, i was driven by apollo to the shrine of artemis,
　　officiated by a woman the age of my sister
pursued, not by furies alone, but by agents of clytemnestra and
　　aegisthus, condemned to death for stealing an effigy of the
　　goddess
but *deus ex machina* intervened, the gods descended on the scene;
　　how else would i have been rescued in a foreign land?

i could not at first imagine but help came when least expected in
　　time, place, and lineage
when i was disrobed for execution, seeing my royal insignia, the
　　priestess yelled! if i could i would have bolted from this scene
　　and her attention-bringing shriek
but seeing again the royal ring of agamemnon on my finger, she
　　signalled silence

going the deductive way she put two and two together to arrive at
　　the revelation that with this royal ring the gods had brought us
　　together,
the ring electra removed from agamemnon's finger the day he
　　died when confusion was wailing in the air
so, electra divines, i am her brother orestes, pursued by the furies
　　and clytemnestra's agents, and it was time to plan a joint return

for she was iphigenia, assumed dead, but saved by goddess
　　artemis and sent to guard her crimean shrine, an incident homer
　　did not reveal:

for him iphigenia was dead but the playwrights did tell: when
the knife was at her throat artemis took pity on my sister and
produced a deer to take her place
then took my sister to the phocis shrine, where my executioner
turned out to be my saviour, blood-tie revealed

4

the recognition scene in every greek play or epic is very emotional,
and so was ours
an appeal to the gods to forgive me was finally made and granted;
iphigenia cleansed me of the power of the furies who, now
transformed into the benign ones, broke the cycle of blood-for-
blood feuds
given a new name and role they become semnai, the venerable
ones, honoured by the citizens of athens

the venerable ones cleansed me as their first duty and i returned
shriven by the gods and goddesses who loved me,
to mycenae to retrieve my throne, restore rule of law, and live an
upright life
to retrieve what was mine and had long been taken away and
besmirched was a daunting task of changing the guards,
assigning them new roles, and keeping the crown firmly on my
head

now all that accomplished, i am restoring good governance as the
people of mycenae have ordained, as well as their apollo-guided
reforms
to recover our standing amongst nations, so the people who
erased troy need not tremble over possible revenge or return to
mismanagement
accepting a belated welcome for my father we now could
broadcast the acceptance speech
my father had written for receiving mycenaean welcome which
my scrupulous sister electra had kept hidden waiting for this
occasion

after being on the run since childhood, i must look for a bride to
share my throne.
now is the time to enjoy happiness and ask who will cook for me,
my guests and sisters when they come back to visit?

my cousin hermione, daughter of helen and menelaus, is just
   the wife for me: the spurious marriage concocted between
   neoptolemus and hermione already betrothed to me does not
   register
thank you god apollo who wants law and communal order, which
   the trojans tried to take from us

5

now that the gods have accepted the matricide i carried out as a
    divine execution,
let it go out loud and clear: don't underrate a child, for he will
    grow up and work his wonders
work to set aright the deeds visited on visited on humanity in his
    youth, deeds done in darkness, dark deeds whose time has come
    for revaluation and correction

let it be said, the revenge the gods back is their rule and that of
    cultural artefacts, material or mental, that have served upright
    people well, as long as they are corrective
you cannot with impunity slay your man and take his cousin to
    the marital bed when he should get his own wife and expand the
    number of relatives
and, having killed, say the case is closed; that's not how to gather
    weeds into a head and bind them together nicely for a bonfire

the cycle of feuding, murder, incestuous cannibalism, rape and
    usurpation must now end
you cannot continue unpunished a chain of evil on grounds of
    feuds
you cannot say fire for fire, ice for ice, disorder is the way of our
    home. no.

since apollo gave us his blessings, the gods on high mount
    olympus
have instituted a regime of moral reformation: no house may feud
if a dark deed is inadvertently committed, let it be recognized as a
    straying, and let amends be made, timeously

the gods on high should convene to reveal the wrongdoer,
    reveal to us as only they know how so that we can institute the
    punishment
if it is payment of compensation may it be done and fast, without
    harassment, and let man on earth accept the divine judgement
    and make it law: received from up, applied down below,
    reported up

the gods' deputies on earth thinking, talking and acting after consulting with their patron gods and clan leaders religiously, cross-culturally and progressively like maasai-karamojong-toposa traditional elders.

1

i orestes, and my friend pylades, first at delphi and then phocis,
    romped our childhood away
we played and played in king strophius' palace, pylades' father
    who had given me protection
when caught with artemis' sacred image on apollo's orders,
    circumstances and coincidence orchestrated the subtext; i was
    sent to be recognized

for this i was to die, but recognition rescued me, for rescued
    iphigenia was the priestess who had to execute me, executioner
    become rescuer
my fiancée hermione loved neoptolemus more and she ran
    off with him, just as her mother had done with paris; does
    waywardness run in that family's blood?
for my own love, for the glory of my name, i needed hermione to
    grace mycenae and the halls of my palace

my father-in-law-to-be had needed a thousand-ship armada to
    rescue his wife but my ways are different; we'll fight it out man
    to man
i had no choice but to kill neoptolemus, that flame-headed son
    of achilles and killer of old man priam. what glory was there in
    killing that dodderer?
and what pride in inheriting andromache, daughter-in-law to
    priam, and afterwards hurling her son astyanax from the trojan
    citadel to death down below?

the love of a man for the woman who is mistress of his heart and
    palace may lead to crimes of passion
and who can gainsay what love can bring? when the heart desires
    too much it behaves as if it already possesses its quarry and is
    then jealous
the gods up there with their synthetic loves cannot judge for they
    know not of pulsing heart and fast flowing blood in heat, not to
    mention testosterone

i was pardoned for killing my mother because the gods judged
motherhood not absolutely necessary for birth
for athena, sprang from the head of zeus, showed child production
did not need a woman, but if athena was conceived through
imagination
should we take images and imageries for real? are we supposed
to take figures of speech as equally authentic in human affairs?
can't we separate essence from resemblance?

when swans' love-making is admired, don't we have the
imagination to embrace the trope?
how could leda not dream this dream of floating sinuous necks
entwined? or the donkey's erect member in action?
when jehovah, the god of the old religion of prejudaism begot
adam with a finger touch was that the symbolisation of birth by
erection and fertilization by sperm ejaculation? and the rest is left
to imagination? then why are we so literal?

the tautological gods – father, son and holy ghost – do not stand
    interrogation; you accept them on faith
appreciation of human ability to craft a saving grace for a mind
    at its tether's end would lead us to hang on a straw to keep
    mankind in bounds of sanity
metaphor accepted as archetype, we compare what does not exist
    with what does not exist but already exists in usual parlance

the gods, so called, taught me to prefabricate so if zeus raped a
    man's wife, a monkey monkeying around or ravaging a woman
    is a story more persuasive
zeus claimed a bright girl as daughter born of his brain, impossible
    but plausible as figures of speech go
so atreus won the kingdom because a meteor streaked from the
    west feigning an east-side setting sun thus wresting pelops's
    crown

grandfather tyndareus stayed with metaphor so my mother
    bettered him with a befuddling figure of speech; god the swan
    planted an egg in leda to hatch into helen
sophists won with rhetoric, for a well-constructed argument
    always trounces truth,
sweet-tasting justification

they call it due process now; we do not care if you killed your wife
    if you can pay the best lawyer
to confuse the judge and jury – or line some pockets and itching
    palms – and the most expensive forensic witness will set you free
she died of natural causes the courtroom gods decreed; truth lives
    in the rich man's pocket

no gods gave the order; love for hermione made me fight and kill
    neoptolemus: it was a fair combat; cosmic justice was with me.
robbers are a law unto themselves, they go after their own desires
    for a man, a woman, a beast, or gold, and don't care who is hurt.

i am baffled: do unto others what you would they do unto you,
   and you might end up a mangled masochist!

that doing what hurts the majority of mankind should be banned
   i also buy wholeheartedly, but maybe by proportion, for all
   cannot be satisfied
shall we make equal number of spoons for sinistrals when they are
   so few and dextrals so many?
if this is human nature, animal nature, where did it start? *taim
   blong taim tambuna*, time before the idea of time was conceived,
   when only fate existed (papua new guinea *tok pitsin*)

but, philosophy or not, man must acknowledge guilt
if the philosopher-poets of old left us a gift it is this:
guilt is a red-light beacon; don't hurl humankind and all that exists
   into the abyss

3

pride sent neoptolemus to take my wife; counter-pride made me
    fight it out with him, but i was ready to
was neoptolemus pitted equally against aged priam? troy had
    fallen: did we achaians need to kill octogenarians?
did we need to hurl hector's infant son down the citadel?

menelaus and helen found that ancient egyptians referred to death
    as 'wasted';
the praying mantis after receiving the sperm of life from the male,
    kills and eats him
perhaps if we were hungry, killing trojans for food would have not
    been wasted sustenance

capitalists impoverish the world; sophistic philosophers give them
    succour for a few donations of their lucre
but a heart that registers an evil deed is nagged by that memory,
    the whitewashing omo of the sophists cannot help, it is haunted
    by the maddening ugliness of the erinyes until it is shrived:
this is what i now teach and urge taught: guilt-feeling will drive
    you towards shriving and cleansing

i rue the day when the gods erased from the record of their laws
    the erinyes, custodians of our guilt records
they who held guilt feelings in the mind and body of the guilty till
    he lost his senses
my hope is for men and women of the future to create erinyes for
    their times, to return fear through memory and remorse, to crave
    cleansing through the ministration of the erinyes

mankind when you have lost all, have only
one last option left, cling to your guilt
guilt will save you from hurtling down the maelstrom

4

neoptolemus knew hermione was betrothed to me, but did a paris
    thing: eloped with her, negating a rebuff from me, which cosmic
    justice grants
it never occurred to him that we had exchanged vows, and her loss
    would pain my heart
he should have empathised with me if sympathy was beyond him

twin children fall out, then come back together, the shared genes
    within them work wordlessly
had neoptolemus come to apologise, he would still be alive: i
    would have forgiven.
so make amends, let him, who has gone astray come, show
    remorse, even at the risk of being killed

remaining silent with guilt locked inside keeps you walking in
    limbo; whenever a man or woman coughs behind you, you fear
    they already know
so become a child, come back to your brother, confess to him who
    might not know confession.
accept chastisement for stepping beyond the pale: they who
    chastise you today await you to do the same to them when they
    have erred.

we pride ourselves on our rise from quadruped to biped; our
    upright walk, prehensile grasp, retentive mind, imagination of
    useful and useless things;
mankind rose from animalkind by our own feeling, sympathizing
    for syn to sym, abhorred receiving pain and abhorred inflicting
    pain
thus did mankind and womankind create ways for ordering
    human life everywhere

when i killed my mother and uncle, anger was in me, feelings of
   pain drove me to it, and a wish to inflict pain
when neoptolemus killed priam unequally, that was a dictate of
   war, but to take my wife-to-be was wrong
i revenged because of counter pride but i felt the erinyes coming in
   my mind

i leave it to future mankind to rehabilitate them

Acknowledgements

I would like to express my thanks to:

Julie Wark, for typing the original manuscript

My daughter, Census Kabang, for typing the last draft.

John Jackson, for final touches on Greek matters as well as writing the Introduction.

Robert Berold, for his scrupulous editing, as well as having the courage to publish this book.

Tinashe Mushakavanhu, for generously sponsoring the production costs of this book.

Emmanuel Tongun, of Dr Philip Tongun Pharmacy, for his generous sponsorship of the costs of the Juba launch printing.

AFTERWORD

Taban lo Liyong

In the summer of 1964, as a political science and sociology student at Howard University in Washington DC, I went for a summer school at the University of North Carolina, in Chapel Hill. One day I felt ill, and shivered for the next four days. The last time I had shivered like that was in 1958 when my beloved nephew passed away in Bobi, 300 miles away. At the time, I was away from home in Mbale, in Uganda. My sisters, mother, father all prayed hard to their ancestors and spirits so that the message would be broken to me more kindly. When death strikes a near kinsman, the loss is felt by those close to him or her through a secret channel of communication. All our people know this. Human beings are like cacti, children are broken off branches: the transplanted cactus, the parent cactus, thousands of miles away, feels the hurt. Break the parent cactus, the separated branch, continents and oceans away, feels the disjuncture.

The telegram bringing the sad news plodded its way from Gulu, Northern Uganda, to Howard University, then to Chapel Hill to report that my dear father had died. It reached me four days later. Soon after that I left studying political science and sociology and went to study literature and writing. This change needs explaining. In my childhood, I had shown great prowess in sculpture. In Bobi where I grew up, there had lived a famous sculptor called Kokorom. He made such exact pictures of people that, Pygmalion-like, the spirits or genii of art considered themselves permanently married to him, and jealously killed any human wife he ever dared to marry. Father had been warned of this and of possible deaths of his future daughters-in-law. He, like the sensible man he was, did not want my artistic foolishness that was invading his household to continue. But now that he was dead, I had the courage to re-embrace art, and literature. When I was younger I had amused myself reading Okot p'Bitek's copies of Homer's *Iliad* and *Odyssey* translated by Alexander Pope, and I could return to Homer's folktales once more.

Homer's world was filled with all sorts of gods and spirits: the wind had names – Aurora, Zephyr, who were in themselves gods.

The Sun, Phoebus, was also Zeus, and the Sun-Force, Apollo, gave rise to the moon, stars, sky, earth, rivers, mountains, birds, and animals. Air was also force, air was what happened to the world when air passed through: typhoon, gale, hurricane, whirlwind, tornado, cyclone. Sun was not scientific sun, a burning ball of gas: it was drought, famine, heat, poor harvest – you knew sun by its beneficial and destructive effects. Thunder was the voice of the sky, and Sky was god, or gods; voice and whip. Earth was mother, Mother Earth, wife of Sky, mother of earthlings. Sky was the abode of the gods, who also sometimes came to rest on our Sudanese/Ethiopian highest hills (in Greece, the only high point worthy of their abode had been Mount Olympus).

I settled myself down to decipher the symbolic language of Homer's two tales.The first was the *Iliad*, the story of the destruction of Ilion/Troy; a destruction, by war, of one state by another, actually of one confederacy by another confederacy. Or of one civilization by another: the pitting of the Achaian/Greek worldview against that of the Trojans. Two ideologies, one civilized, the other rustic: refinement versus brute force: breeders of beauty versus breeders of horses. Achaia had Helen, paragon of beauty; Troy had beautiful horses. Troy, it seems, was getting fed up riding horses: however beautiful the waves of their tail hair and manes, horses are still horses.

A handsome prince of Troy decided to grace the Trojan palace with the most beautiful possession of Achaia: Queen Helen herself. Of course, beauty cannot be virgin: if it was, Greek mythology would have given beauty its own tragic end like the Titanic. This Achaian beauty was already married to Prince Menelaus, the brother of King Agamemnon: she hung in their palace gallery, so to speak, like a treasured masterpiece. Prince Paris of Troy had to sneak in as a house-guest and, with his band of kidnappers, carry her off on their swift-moving horses to Troy. This too had been prophesied: that he would ignite the fire that would burn Troy to the ground. Banished in childhood by his parents he had, like Oedipus, grown up elsewhere, only to return with the red-hot brand that would fulfill the prophecy.

To have refined their taste to reach the level of nurturing the utmost beauty, would have taken the Achaians thousands of years and heartaches. How could Troy hope to become cultured overnight? How could the raiding, grabbing, snatching of Helen confer upon them the title of refinement? Did they think they would enjoy the fruits of Achaian civilization without sweating, without shedding tears, gnashing teeth? Can a palace be civilized and a state call itself civilized while its populace and countryside is barbaric? For ten years Troy was to learn refinement of taste by enjoying one simple work of art: the masterpiece of Greek culture, Helen.

Surely a people who could produce a paragon of beauty would also possess the means to outwit barbarians, fly-by-night wife-snatchers? Didn't Achaians have the brains, wiliness, bags-of-tricks, to recover their treasured artwork? Even if it took ten years, Achaia was not going to give up; Achaia was going to prove her superiority in matters of love and war. I had realized after the first five pages of the *Iliad*, when the storyteller characterizes Achaia's refinement and Troy's crudeness, that Troy was going to be defeated. After that I read the story in order to hear Homer reveal to me the qualities Achaians held most dear. Their morals and mores were strewn all over the book.

The king is the guardian of the state's values. He cannot allow a robber to take away a dear possession of Achaia without mobilising the whole state and its allies to go and recover it. The honour of Achaia had to be recovered, even at the cost of camping outside Troy for ten years. Even if for ten years the Trojans held them at bay, frustrated them. Even if for ten years Achaians had no clue about how to storm Troy, or prepare their ships for sailing (Achaia was refined enough to make very good ships).

Sacrifices had to be made: to raise the wind to sail the ships, the king had to lose something very dear to him, his daughter, to appease one of the gods to relent and allow the wind that would come to blow the Achaian fighters towards Troy. And the king was not so powerful that he could take away Achilles's slave-wife and not suffer the repercussions. As a result Achilles refused to go to fight: he, the only one who could defeat the Trojans. And while he was sulking, nursing his anger, the Trojans killed plenty of Achaians.

How does one arouse an angry, brooding man to go out to fight? Patroklos, a friend of Achilles, wearing Achilles's armour which was heavier than he could bear, went out to wreak havoc on the

Trojans. After their initial terror, the Trojans realized that the foe was a pretender, regained heart, and killed him. Only then, to revenge the death of his bosom friend, did Achilles go out to fight and put an end to the war. To fight his war, his last war. For friendship's sake.

We have a saying that if you throw down an elephant in a wrestling match, your chest will pain. All generals have to be reminded that they are not immortals; they all have an Achilles heel through which they can be brought down. The rivalry between Achaia and Troy ended. The Trojans were driven away: Aeneas carried Anchises, his aged father, on his back as one of the cultural accoutrements of old Troy which would have to be transplanted in the new Roman soil. Achaia can therefore claim the paternity of the Roman empire which later on swallowed her up. That very fact moved western civilization forward. Blame Helen and her beauty, Paris and his eye for the beautiful.

Perhaps the Romans read only the *Aeneid*, the story of the defeated Trojan Greek Aeneas who went to set up a new civilization in Rome, and never bothered to read the *Odyssey*, about the most successful, artful, of all Achaians, and how he made his catabasis, his return journey, back from Troy. Rome was built on power, force, little philosophy, little heart-searching. Introspection came later, perhaps only with Lucretius and Marcus Aurelius.

When the war started, Odysseus did not want to go to fight. He put self-preservation first. He dressed up like a woman and began grain-winnowing and grinding like an Achaian woman. They went and threshed him out of there. Next, he pretended that he was mad. He sowed salt instead of wheat in his field and went ploughing his new 'seed'. The bluff was soon discovered. They laid his own son Telemachus on the furrow. To see if he was really mad, they ordered Odysseus to cut him to pieces with his plough. Of course he didn't. He was taken to the warfront.

During the war, he was sent to scout – he had the presence of mind to infiltrate enemy lines, create some havoc, and come back alive. He might not have been the best of warriors: that role was reserved for Achilles. But it is not the spear-master only who wins the war. Odysseus knew how to coordinate the war effort, and he invented the Trojan Horse and infiltrated it into the enemy territory. Wiles matter. Odysseus's father was a renowned robber, a thief if you like. Famous or notorious, in Greek mythology. Perhaps planning and carrying out daring deeds of plunder ran in the family.

After the war, the hero has to return home. No matter how long it takes, no matter the distractions he meets on the way – Circe, the Sirens, the island of Calypso – the hero has to return home. And no other home is more civilized than Achaia, no wife more lovely than Penelope, no son so dear as Telemachus.

The *Odyssey* is the catabasis (descent, return) as the *Iliad* was the anabasis (ascent, going forward) of the last of the Achaian Troy-destroyers. Odysseus was the Achaians' *primus inter pares*, and his story had therefore to be told in order to remind future Achaians of their best civic qualities, their best cultural qualities, and their dictum: survive at all costs. *A luta continua*. His father had waited for him: he did not die when his son was away. His wife kept all suitors at bay by weaving the shroud by day and undoing it by night, a ruse for maintaining her fidelity. Telemachus, outnumbered as he was by would-be stepfathers, kept faith in his father's ability to triumph over all foreign dangers and eventually to return. Odysseus's dog Argus was the first to recognize the return of his master, and died of joy. His wet-nurse, kept alive all this time for her epic role, almost blurted out the identity of the enigmatic guest she was bathing when she recognized the scar on his right thigh. Father, son, and servants destroyed all the suitors who had been eating them out of house and home.

This national hero of Achaia, Odysseus, is a complex character. Pragmatic as he is, he will lie, cheat, and murder for the sake of Achaia, and return to her. Everything Odysseus does in the *Iliad* and the *Odyssey* points to the qualities Achaians approved in their heroes: duty to the state first, second, and third. Fight all gods and men, adopt temporary peace or truces with gods, goddesses, spirits, men and women: anything to get what you want.

In Penelope resides the quality of the Achaian public woman: faithful to her husband, gentle but firm in discouraging suitors, clever enough to make up stories to protect her virtue. Married early, then left to tend little Telemachus, the wife of a soldier missing in action, she was besieged by Achaia's best suitors – the men who do not go to war but feast on the heroes' wealth.

Picture the evening when Odysseus, his son Telemachus, and his shepherds and house servants had just killed all the suitors, including Antinoos, who was generous and would have been the one favoured by Penelope had Odysseus not returned. Imagine Odysseus that evening, tired from the carnage, sitting in the hall with his war gear and bloody hands. Look now at Penelope trying to reconcile herself to the inevitable: this stranger, whoever he is, now demands to be accepted as her Odysseus back from war. But she has a final test to put to the stranger, the test which will reveal to her whether the man in front of her is an imposter or not. In my poem I verbalize Penelope's silent thoughts, follow the thread of her musings.

Since Odysseus has to overcome all obstacles, he has to have ready answers to all problems, sometimes with the help of gods, goddesses, or spirits. Most times his ways were immoral. If we were not predisposed towards him, we would find many reasons to blame him for unvirtuous decisions and actions. But, of course, we all love a hero. And we, now living in our Christian era, should remember that the Greek epics were collected centuries after they were assumed to have happened (if ever) in pagan Western Asia or the Aegean sea. We cannot use our yardsticks to judge them.

How do those who call themselves the heirs of Greek civilization view this war between these East (Ilion/Troy) versus West (Achaia/Greece) confederacies? How do they regard the Greek gods and goddesses – fickle, capricious, vengeful, and exacters of heavy payment when one wants to mollify them? Do they revere them, or look at them my way, with an African folklorist's mentality?

The tradition-bound African reader is at an advantage here, being orally-tuned to storytelling, receiving and conceiving events told in the oral way and by still being pagan or semi-pagan. His morality-domain is still Solomonic, or dominated by the morality of 'an eye for an eye' ethics, whether in my nation of South Sudan or in lands as far away as Papua New Guinea. I used to argue against the concept of time warp but now understand it properly. For example we Kuku originated from two sources: West Africa Mali with whom we share some words for numerals and East Africa Maasai with whom we share some of the remaining words for numerals. The rinderpest of the 1800's depleted our cattle. So we moved west, first to Dongotono then to Kajo Keji. There we became settled mixed peasants, cultivators. The colonialists prevailed on us there. In 1926 my own grand-uncle, Chief Boso, invited British educators to come to modernise us. Engineer Barnaba Dumo and I were among the first batch of Kuku graduates. In the same way in Papua New Guinea, the coastal Papuans were modernised first, and the highland New Guineans, like the South Sudanese Sudd-dwellers, are still struggling to catch up. I can't see the time warp here. It was the opportunity catchers who stuck on blindly who benefitted.

If one is the upholder of unbending rules, like Plato, or like Heraklitus who rebuked Homer for not taking a moral stance on some of Odysseus's cheating strategies, one would find good reasons for condemning all literary creations in which winning-at-all-costs is the way of the hero. Works in which there is no censuring of immoral thoughts and deeds, in which spurious arguments are used for the sake of winning a case – in short, where sophistry rules the day. These would include all fictions where the hero loses to the villain till the end when a knock-out blow is begrudged the hero.

Of course Odysseus had elaborate and more sophisticated ways for winning the obstacles placed on his way. He had an answer for any and every problem. In a lower key, the sophists did the same in tackling matters in court which, they, rather than Socrates should have been convicted for.

Since we now live in the 21st century we need to be relativistic. This is where the concept of paradigm shift comes in: stand firmly in your century but also cast your mind backwards to those events which supposedly took place in the 'pagan' world of Greece 4 000 years ago. Make allowances for the level of 'civilization' and its different morality then. If your culture is more Christian then you will be approaching the past through the tinted glasses of Christianity, or whatever is your religious approach to life. Many epochs have passed, and humanity everywhere has faced similar existential problems. What were these problems called, in the eras before ours? Are we not meeting problems our ancestors met before us? Why are we now struggling with creating new names for them which our tongues can pronounce but our minds struggle to conceive? Isn't that what we mean when we say 'the Greeks had a name for it'?

Whose world is closer to the world in which Odysseus travelled – the Amazon forest Indian and his so-called 'primitive culture', or the Chimbu man in the Uplands of Papua New Guinea, or the South Sudanese riverine folk in the Sudd who have never seen a white man, or the New Yorker munching a complicated sandwich, reading his favourite magazine while also drinking his coffee? Between an African undergraduate student of Greek literature and a European student of Greek literature who would comprehend those ancient events more readily? The pagan or semi-pagan African has the advantage. Richard Wright, though he was an African American, caught a tail of it in Spain in his 1950s book *Pagan Spain*. The 'pagan' world in which we still live contains features of the world of classical Greece and the other countries of the southern Mediterranean, worlds that Odysseus was to look for in his last Odyssey, people who would mistake his oar for a winnowing implement. Perhaps those countries should accept membership of the Third World and join us in plotting our way up the development ladder together.

If you follow the story carefully, you will notice that Greek philosophical morality has changed by the end of it. It starts from Penelope's home-grown identity tests on her husband; then Clytemnestra's long-nursed grudge against her husband for slaughtering their daughter; prior to that, it started when God Zeus planted his seed of life through a swan to produce Miss Greece, Helen; the story is pushed forward by code-of-hospitality-breaker, Paris; leading to the thousand-ship 'rescue squadron' armada to retrieve King Menelaus' wayward wife; not forgetting Achilles's mega-sulk for the deprivation of his war-booty by Supreme Commander Agamemnon; by the time the tenth year of camping outside Troy had been reached and victory won, the double-murder in the bathtub was accomplished, and Orestes, with his friend Pylades, was grown up and ready to avenge the murder of his father by his mother and her paramour (also his uncle) Aegisthus; this was followed by Apollo's rebuke and the deprivation of the powers of punishment against matricide by the Furies/Erinyes; it ends in Orestes killing Achilles's son, Neoptolemus, in a royal duel.

At the beginning of the story King Menelaus's wife has been 'kidnapped' by a young prince from the next kingdom. Instead of his going well-armed and fighting the culprit, he resorts to the ready-formed mechanism of the Achaian confederacy. The armada stays put for nine years because a seer says so. And they camp outside Troy for those nine whole years. Achilles had his concubine snatched by the king and leader of the confederacy, Agamemnon. He, the leading spear-master, does not challenge the robber to a personal duel. Tradition is against it.

By the end of these ups and downs the morality had changed. Penelope, housewife, mother, wife, presumed widow, most desired upper-class widow of her time, would now spend the whole evening cogitating whether the guest before her was indeed her man. She no longer trusted culture and the gods and tradition that had ruled her before. There was a litany of questions she had to go through before assuring herself that the carpetbagger before her was indeed Odysseus.

We have this new scenario: whilst King Agamemnon is pursuing the destruction of Troy, Clytemnestra is orchestrating his destruction on his arrival. Gender roles, traditional respect for husband and gods, go to hell. She will remember them when pleading her case after the event. If at all it ever comes to pass.

Iphigenia is being sacrificed by her father. Some playwrights report that one of the gods substituted a deer, and whisked her away to be a priestess elsewhere, awaiting service to her brothers in another land and time.

Since God Zeus 'bore' Athene out of his head, God Apollo himself descends on the stage and pleads in the highest court that even human beings do not need a mother to be born! He defends Orestes, demanding that the Erinyes therefore stop harassing and persecuting Orestes for killing his mother. Does that mean matricide is now alright?

Orestes was already betrothed to Hermione, Helen and Menelaus's daughter. But red-headed Achilles's son Neoptolemus decided to flee with her the way Paris had done with her mother. How does Orestes answer this provocation? Not as his uncle had done. For him this was a something that faced two people. Let a duel settle it. He kills Neoptolemus in that duel and ends the matter there and then.

If, in my study of these classical Greek literary works, I call this present endeavour an investment in the stock market of Troy, what then are my returns? These are my unaudited results:

In all of these turbulences, I see a contest between traditionalism and modernism. In Homer's time it was traditionalism that ruled supreme. But in Socrates' time traditionalism was being shaken, and the political powers-that-were did not like it. They were against those worshipping and teaching new gods and beliefs. These were corruptors of youth, they said, and they zeroed in on those who were, like Socrates, supposedly professing belief in new gods. In truth it was the Sophists they should have pursued. This was the wind of change blowing in the philosophically awakened world of the Mediterranean Sea.

What I see coming out of the Troy story is a new awakening for humanity. Instead of Penelope relying on the gods she seeks personal assurance; instead of going to consult the auguries she is making up her own mind and taking action. Here we see man (or woman) making up their mind and being prepared to bear the consequences. For Orestes, there is no more recourse to a confederacy or a god or a tradition. Nor to a legal game like that of the sophists. At least the Greek gods of that time also participate in human life and change their minds (though mankind may never agree with their new versions of laws).

One realizes that legal sophistry was the successor religion to sophism, and the death of Socrates the introduction of a new kind of religion. One then has to skilfully separate Socratism from sophism. Socrates has his spirits, genies which communicate with him personally. His spirits were personal, not collective. Still, Aristophanes and other playwrights wanted to cash in on the popularity of a spoof on Socrates at the box-office. That the judgment was a mistrial is not a reflection on Socrates.

But what does making up one's mind and standing by the consequences mean? When Orestes challenges Neoptolemus to a combat whose result could go either way, he is staking his all on it. Besides, he did not have to consult Apollo. But if one's desires and one's might now decide the issue, then how can a weaker actor win the case? And how can that weakness be ameliorated to serve the just man, that is, the man for whom a better case could be made? For moral judgment to be part of it, the legal system the world over should contribute jurists believing in humanism. They will have to draw up a new legal system. That system will return justice to where it was when the sophists derailed it and caused Socrates to die; and it would draw up laws for challenging the dominance of sophism in the legal and economic fields. For a long time it only showed its presence in morality and ethics, but I think the time is not far off when man will take charge of his future and the future of the world without asking for permission from traditions or religions or the gods. That is what I would call modernist Humanism.

Do I read the Greeks right? Was the wind of change there? Tough sophism was strong, but wasn't humanism also on the cards? Then why was Socrates sentenced to drink the hemlock? Am I making a premature prognostication? Audit me and then compare my returns against the given offers and the market performance generally. I would rather make a guess in the right direction than accept the continued stay or growth of the present poppery, twittery and trumpery.

In conclusion, may I introduce to you the maiden Nausicaa. She who welcomed a raft-blown stranger to her portion of a river, had her girls wash him, oil him, and serve him food and wine. Then coached him on how to approach her father and on how to behave in court. He followed all her instructions and came out with flying colours. She was such a good influence on the usually crafty Odysseus.

The highlights of this visit were: Odysseus's discovery of and reception by the girls; his welcoming by the fire; the bantering and sports competition; the musical recital and the storytelling of incidents of the *Iliad*; the competition to see who gave better or costlier gifts than the king. When a self-driving ship was ready to take Odysseus home, the king had all his presents loaded in a chest.

If all visits went like these, one could make visiting a daily routine. Perhaps not an everyday routine, perhaps a daily celebration of humanity will do! But could a visitor for whom one's assistance yielded so much not find a way for meeting and thanking the host publicly? (Nausicaa did find a little space to remind him, but according to me, she deserved a public acknowledgement).

Perhaps we men (and some women too) do not understand womankind very much. Perhaps we men take the women's side too lightly. Many times women see us bungling matters, and chuckle inside themselves. And Odysseus, who never cared how much Penelope agonised through the decision to accept him or not as her man, does not take the initiative in letting the whole court give Nausicaa a pat on the back. Bearing in mind this all happened over 3 000 years ago.

Now, whether it is in African folktales or the same story, after hearing both stories twice, one selects one's favourite. So in Book Two of this book, I give you the reader both versions of Telemachus's and Odysseus's stories. My Helen, Cassandra, Agamemnon, Clytemnestra and Orestes are original creatures. They are creatures of modernism or post-modernism.

****

Today I am looking forward to a huge calabash of my favourite brew of kwete from MamaAfrika. I shall drink it frothing hot. For it was demanded of me by the Aleppo Elders that I should finish writing this book which I spent many evenings composing. When I finished writing it, MamaAfrika was to be informed beforehand so that the spirits of Okot p'Bitek, Can Themba, Es'kia Mphahlele, Dambudzo Marechera, Amos Tutuola, Chinua Achebe, Aimé Césaire, Leopold Sedar Senghor, would join us from the other world in celebrating its immortal birth. My father and mother would have their sitting of the elders. I am sure they will enjoy the company.

Thank you very much for your present company.

Printed in the United States
By Bookmasters